A QUICK COURSE® IN

QUATTRO® PRO
For Windows™

A QUICK COURSE® IN

QUATTRO® PRO
For Windows™

JOYCE COX

PATRICK KERVRAN

AN ONLINE PRESS BOOK

PUBLISHED BY
Online Press Incorporated
14320 NE 21st Street, Suite 18
Bellevue, WA 98007
(206) 641-3434
(800) 854-3344

Copyright © 1992 by Online Press Inc.

All rights reserved. No part of the contents of this book may be reproduced or transmitted in any form or by any means without the written permission of the publisher.

Publisher's Cataloging in Publication
(prepared by Quality Books Inc.)

Cox, Joyce K., 1946–
   A quick course in Quattro Pro for windows / Joyce K. Cox,
Patrick Kervran.
     p. cm.
     Includes index.
     ISBN 1-879399-11-3
   1. Quattro pro (computer program) 2. Electronic spreadsheets —
computer programs. 3. Windows (computer programs)   I. Kervran,
Patrick, 1961– II. Title.

HF5548.4.Q39C6 1992	650'.0285'5369
	QBI91-2015
	91-68448
	CIP

Printed and bound in the United States of America

1 2 3 4 5 6 7 8 9 T N Z P 3 2 1 0

Distributed to bookstores by Publishers Group West (800) 788-3123

Quick Course® is a registered trademark of Online Press Inc. Quattro® is a registered trademark of Borland International Inc. Windows™ is a trademark and Microsoft® is a registered trademark of Microsoft Corporation. All other products mentioned in this book are trademarks of their respective owners.

Contents

Introduction vi

1 Building a Simple Notebook 1

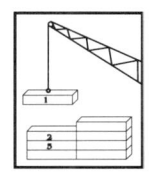

To learn the basics of Quattro Pro, we build a simple table for tracking sales by invoice. We show you how to get information into Quattro Pro, how to edit and format it, and how to save and retrieve files.

2 Analyzing Income 32

There's no better way to take the mystery out of Quattro Pro than to dive right in. As you learn how to perform calculations on the sales data, you'll think of many things you can analyze in similar ways.

3 Extracting Information from a Database 62

Databases are a snap with Quattro Pro. Our step-by-step examples show how to sort and extract data. Then we use powerful yet efficient Quattro Pro database @functions to perform calculations on data subsets.

4 Tracking Budgets 88

There's little joy in tracking budgets, but Quattro Pro's sophisticated graphing capabilities help you analyze budget components by displaying them visually in a variety of formats on the notebook page or as separate graphics.

5 Estimating Project Costs 108

First, we build a set of independent notebooks that can be used for many purposes. Then we link them and look up information needed to prepare bids for clients or allocate in-house resources.

6 Quattro Pro Macros 124

Quattro Pro's formatting capabilities are showcased as we build an invoice. In the process, we show how to use macros to automate common tasks. Then we examine a macro that transfers data from the invoice to a notebook that tracks sales.

Index 140

Introduction

It's been a long time coming, but people are saying it's been worth the wait. Quattro® Pro for Windows™ is here at last!

Whether you've just purchased a copy of this innovative new spreadsheet program, your boss has purchased a copy for you, or you're thinking about purchasing a copy, we're here to show you how to use it.

In this book, we get right to the heart of Quattro® Pro and show you how to create real-life spreadsheet notebooks that you can put directly to use in your business.

We start in Chapter 1 by creating a notebook that records sales, and then we show you how to manipulate the information in the notebook in various ways. In Chapters 2 and 3, we continue working with the notebook from Chapter 1, gradually building experience with basic procedures and progressing to more advanced techniques. You should read these first three chapters in sequence, being careful to save your notebooks when we tell you to so that you have what you need for future tasks.

You can read the last three chapters in any order, because each chapter focuses on a different topic and uses independent notebooks. In Chapter 4, we use a simple budget notebook to explore outlining and charting. In Chapter 5, we build a notebook for estimating project costs and create links to two other notebooks so that the totals account for indirect as well as direct costs. And in Chapter 6, we show how to define formatting styles and write macros to speed up the process of creating an invoice. We end the chapter by examining a macro that transfers information from the invoice to a sales log—creating a notebook that is similar to the one we built in Chapters 1, 2, and 3.

In designing our notebooks, we have made each one general enough to be adapted easily to other business tasks, and in several chapters we suggest other situations in which the notebooks might apply. In this book, as in all *Quick Course*® books, we have scattered handy tips and useful tidbits throughout each chapter so that when you have the time, you can look them over and learn even more about this new Windows™ version of Quattro® Pro. For those times when you need to refer back to a particular discussion or want to browse ahead, we use arrows and captions to draw your attention to key information and procedures so that you can easily spot them later on as you thumb through the book.

With that said, let's move on to Chapter 1 and start taking advantage of the many exciting features Quattro® Pro for Windows™ has to offer.

Building a Simple Notebook

Getting Oriented..2
Entering Text 4
Entering Numeric Values..9
Entering Dates and Times..10
Selecting Blocks..11
Giving Quattro Pro Instructions..13
Object Inspectors 14
The SpeedBar..14
Keyboard Shortcuts..15
Saving Notebooks 15
Creating New Notebooks...16
Manipulating Windows..17
Editing Basics 19
Changing Entries..19
Copying Entries 19
Moving Entries..22
Clearing Cells..23
Inserting and Deleting Cells..24
Formatting Basics 26
Changing Notebook Formatting 26
Changing Column Widths..28
Getting Help..30
Quitting Quattro Pro 31

Cell addresses
Page 4

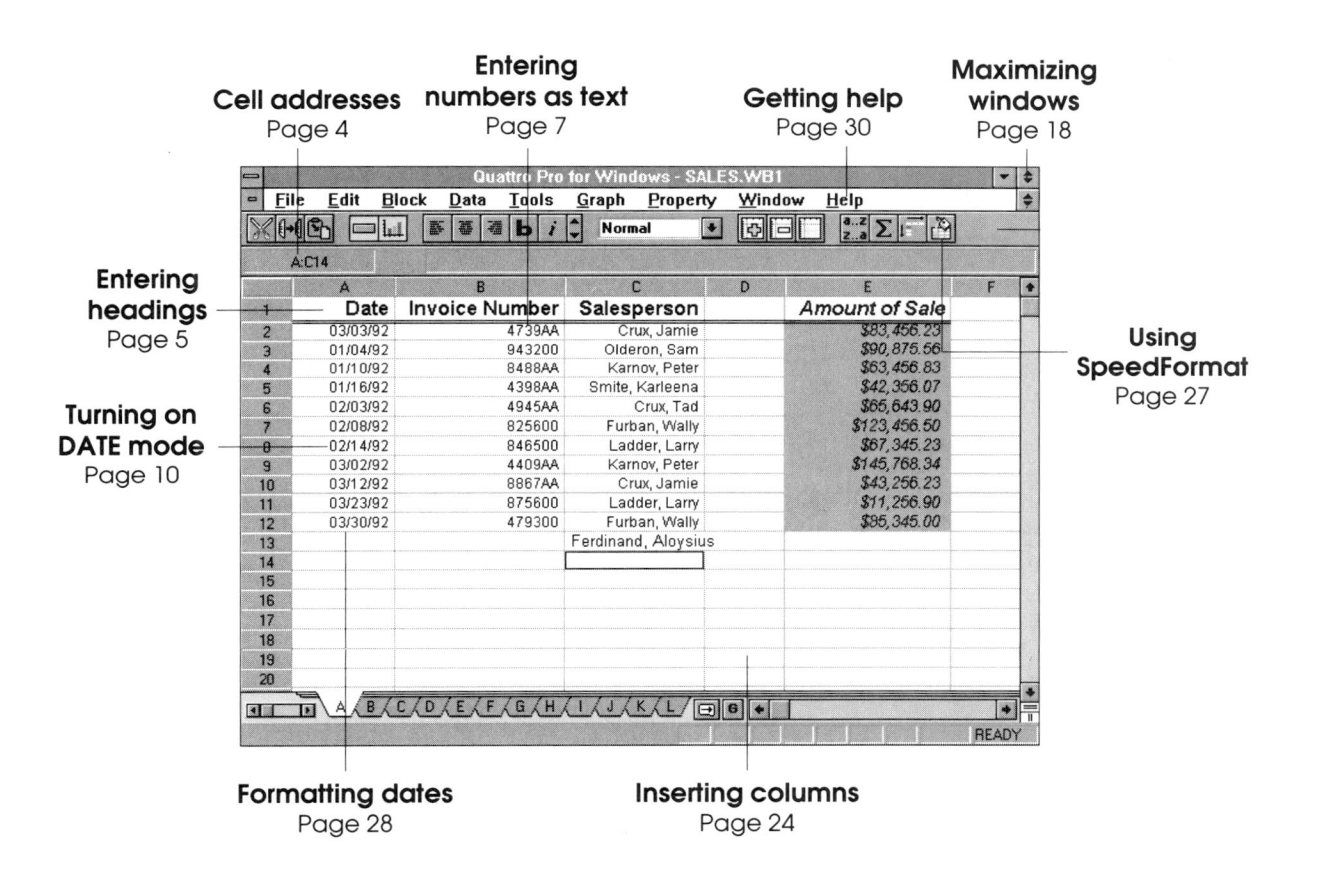

Entering numbers as text
Page 7

Getting help
Page 30

Maximizing windows
Page 18

Entering headings
Page 5

Turning on DATE mode
Page 10

Using SpeedFormat
Page 27

Formatting dates
Page 28

Inserting columns
Page 24

	A	B	C	D	E	F
1	Date	Invoice Number	Salesperson		Amount of Sale	
2	03/03/92	4739AA	Crux, Jamie		$83,456.23	
3	01/04/92	943200	Olderon, Sam		$90,875.56	
4	01/10/92	8488AA	Karnov, Peter		$63,456.83	
5	01/16/92	4398AA	Smite, Karleena		$42,356.07	
6	02/03/92	4945AA	Crux, Tad		$65,643.90	
7	02/08/92	825600	Furban, Wally		$123,456.50	
8	02/14/92	846500	Ladder, Larry		$67,345.23	
9	03/02/92	4409AA	Karnov, Peter		$145,768.34	
10	03/12/92	8867AA	Crux, Jamie		$43,256.23	
11	03/23/92	875600	Ladder, Larry		$11,256.90	
12	03/30/92	479300	Furban, Wally		$85,345.00	
13			Ferdinand, Aloysius			

Quattro Pro for Windows - SALES.WB1

A:C14

READY

You're probably sitting at your computer, anxious to start crunching numbers. But before we get going, we need to cover some basics, such as how to enter text and numbers, save files, move around a spreadsheet (called a notebook in Quattro Pro), edit and format entries, and print the results of your labors. After we discuss a few fundamentals, you'll easily be able to create the spreadsheets and graphs we cover in the rest of the book.

We assume that you've already installed both Windows 3.1 or a later version and Quattro Pro for Windows on your computer. We also assume that you've worked with Windows before and that you know how to start programs, move windows, choose commands from menus, highlight text, and so on. If you're a Windows novice, we recommend that you take a look at *A Quick Course in Windows*, another book in the Quick Course series, which will help you quickly come up to speed.

To follow the instructions in this book, you should be using a mouse. Although it is theoretically possible to work in Windows and Quattro Pro using just the keyboard, we would not wish that fate on anyone, and most of our instructions involve using a mouse. Occasionally, however, when it is easier or faster to use the keyboard, we give the keyboard equivalent of the mouse action.

Starting Quattro Pro

Well, let's get going. With the DOS prompt (C:>) on your screen, start Windows by typing *win* and pressing Enter. Then, in Windows, start Quattro Pro by double-clicking the Quattro Pro icon in the Quattro Pro For Windows group window.

Getting Oriented

When you start Quattro Pro for the first time, your screen looks something like the one on the facing page. At the top of the screen is the Quattro Pro for Windows title bar, followed by the menu bar, from which you choose commands. Below the menu bar is the SpeedBar, a Quattro Pro feature that puts a host of often-used buttons within easy reach. Below the SpeedBar is the input line, in which you enter the values (text and numbers) and formulas that you'll use in your spreadsheets.

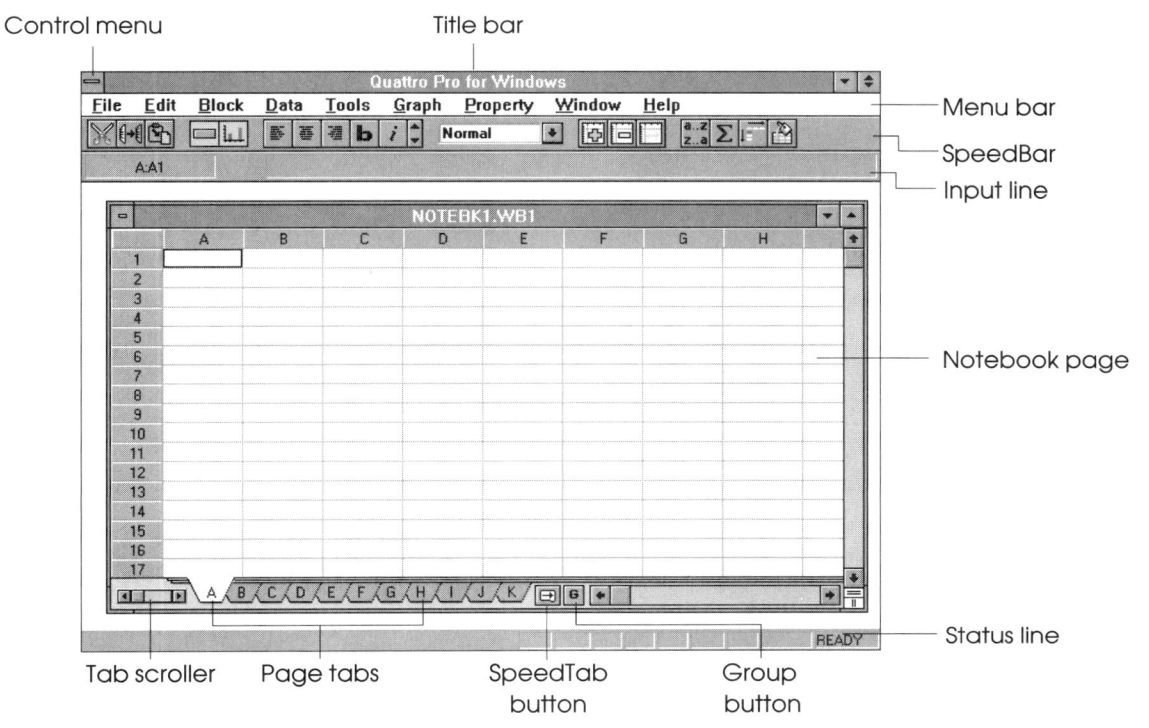

Chapter 1 Building a Simple Notebook

Screen element labels: Control menu, Title bar, Menu bar, SpeedBar, Input line, Notebook page, Status line, Tab scroller, Page tabs, SpeedTab button, Group button.

Taking up the majority of the screen is the first blank spreadsheet. Each spreadsheet is one page in a 256-page notebook, with an extra page especially for graphs. The name of this notebook, NOTEBK1.WB1, appears in the title bar of the notebook window. As you can see, the notebook page is laid out in a grid of columns and rows like the ledger paper used by accountants. The rectangle at the junction of each column and row is called a cell. Each cell has an address

Other ways of starting

To start Quattro Pro (or any other Windows program) directly from the DOS prompt, type *win*, a space, and the program's filename. For Quattro Pro, type *win qpw*, and press Enter. Windows locates Quattro Pro, bypassing the Windows Program Manager. You can also start Quattro Pro with a notebook already loaded by typing *win qpw*, a space, and the name of the notebook.

Missing Quattro Pro group?

The Quattro Pro installation program creates the Quattro Pro For Windows group by default. If you do not see this group in Program Manager, someone might have moved the Quattro Pro icon and deleted the Quattro Pro For Windows group. Open the other group windows (Applications is a likely candidate), locate the Quattro Pro icon, and double-click it to start the program.

The SpeedBar and status line

If you do not see the SpeedBar or the status line, click the Quattro Pro For Windows title bar with the right mouse button to open the application Object Inspector, select the Show SpeedBar and Show Status Line options, and then click OK.

Cell addresses

that consists of the letter displayed in the border at the top of the cell's column and the number displayed in the border at the left end of its row. For example, the address of the cell in the top-left corner of the spreadsheet is A1. The address of the cell below A1 is A2, and the address of the cell to the right of A1 is B1. Quattro Pro displays the address of the active cell—the one you are currently working with—in the cell indicator at the left end of the input line.

Notebook statistics

The notebook page has 256 columns, lettered A through IV, and 8192 rows, numbered 1 through 8192. The 256 notebook pages are also labeled A through IV. This works out to be a total of over 500 million cells, large enough for just about any set of calculations, short of the national budget.

You use the window's horizontal and vertical scroll bars to scroll cells into view. To display a different notebook page, click the Rolodex-like page tabs at the bottom of the window, or use the small tab scroller next to the page tabs to scroll notebook pages into view. To the right of the page tabs is the SpeedTab button, which you can click to instantly turn to the Graphs page located at the end of the notebook. To the right of the SpeedTab button is the Group button, which you use when you want to make changes to several pages at once in Group mode. (Don't worry about these buttons for now; we'll show you how they work later.)

At the bottom of the screen is the status line, which displays the Quattro Pro mode indicators, useful information about menu and button selections, and the status of keys, such as whether Num Lock or Caps Lock is turned on. At the moment, Quattro Pro displays READY to indicate that it is ready for you to do something.

Entering Text

Most notebooks consist of blocks of text and numbers in table format on which you can perform various calculations. To make the tables easy to decipher, you usually give the columns and rows labels that describe their associated entries. Let's try entering a few labels now:

1. On the blank notebook page, check that cell A1 is selected (click it if it isn't). The dark border, called the selector, surrounds cell A1 to indicate that it is the active cell, meaning that anything you type will appear there.

2. Type *Date*. As you type, the characters are displayed in the input line. A blinking insertion point leads the way, telling you where the next character you type will be inserted. The ✓ and X buttons appear to the left of the input line. Meanwhile, the indicator in the status line changes from READY to LABEL, indicating that Quattro Pro recognizes the entry as a text label. ← **Entering headings**

3. Click the ✓ button to record the entry. Quattro Pro displays the Date label in cell A1, and the indicator in the status line changes back to READY. Notice that the text is left-aligned in its cell. Unless you tell Quattro Pro to do otherwise, it always left-aligns labels and right-aligns numbers. In the input line, you'll see that Quattro Pro has put an apostrophe (')—its left-alignment label prefix—before the label. ← **Recording entries with the ✓ button**

4. Click cell B1 to select it. The selector moves one cell to the right, and the address in the cell indicator changes from A:A1 to A:B1, indicating that cell B1 of notebook page A is now active.

5. Type *Invoice Number*, but instead of clicking the ✓ button to record the label in the cell, press the Right Arrow key. Quattro Pro displays the entry in cell B1 and moves the selector to C1.

6. Type *Salesperson*, and press Right Arrow.

7. Now enter one more label. In cell D1, type *Amount of Sale*, and click the ✓ button to record the entry. Here's how the spreadsheet looks with the newly entered row of labels:

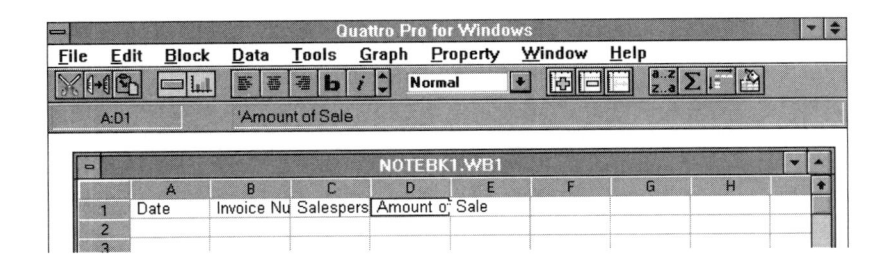

Long text entries

Notice that the labels in cells B1, C1, and D1 are too long to fit in their cells. Until you entered the Salesperson label in cell C1, the Invoice Number label spilled over into C1, just as Amount of Sale now spills over from D1 into E1. After you entered the Salesperson label, Quattro Pro truncated Invoice Number so that you could read the label in C1. Similarly, after you entered Amount of Sale, Quattro Pro truncated Salesperson. The Invoice Number and Salesperson labels are still intact in B1 and C1, however. (If you're skeptical, click either cell and look at the input line.) In a minute, you'll learn how to adjust column widths to accommodate long entries.

That's it for the column labels. Now let's turn our attention to the rest of the table. We'll skip the Date and Invoice Number columns for the moment and enter the names of a few salespeople in last-name/first-name order in column C.

1. Click cell C2 to select it, and type *Crux, Jamie*.

2. Instead of clicking the ✓ button, click cell C3. Quattro Pro records the entry in cell C2 and makes cell C3 the active cell.

3. Type *Olderon, Sam* in cell C3, and press Down Arrow to record the entry and move to cell C4.

4. Next, type the following names in the Salesperson column, pressing Down Arrow after each one:

   C4   Karnov, Peter
   C5   Smite, Karleena

Mouse pointer shapes

The mouse pointer takes on different shapes depending on where it is on the screen. For example, the pointer is an arrow when it is over the notebook page, the menu bar, the SpeedBar, or the title bar; a double-headed arrow when it is over a column or row border; and an I-beam when it is in the input line in EDIT mode.

Correcting mistakes

If you make a mistake when entering information in your notebook, you can correct the error by selecting the cell containing the error and pressing the F2 function key to activate the input line. Then use the following keys to move the insertion point and edit the contents:

Home or **End** moves the insertion point to the beginning or end of the entry.
Right Arrow or **Left Arrow** moves the insertion point forward or backward one character.
Backspace or **Delete** deletes the character before or after the insertion point.
Esc deletes the contents of the input line. (Pressing Esc again restores the cell's original contents and leaves the cell active.)
Clicking the **X** button cancels any current changes, restores the original contents, and leaves the cell active.

C6   Crux, Tad
C7   Furban, Wally
C8   Ladder, Larry
C9   Karnov, Peter
C10   Crux, Jamie
C11   Ladder, Larry
C12   Furban, Wally

Now let's enter some invoice numbers in column B. Usually, you will want Quattro Pro to treat invoice numbers—and Social Security numbers, part numbers, phone numbers, and other numbers that are used primarily for identification—as text rather than as numeric values on which you might want to perform calculations. If a label contains digits, you have to explicitly tell Quattro Pro to treat it as text. (If a number includes characters such as hyphens, Quattro Pro attempts to compute the entry as a formula. For example, Quattro Pro views Social Security numbers, such as 145-34-6476, as subtraction equations.)

Entering numbers as text

For demonstration purposes, assume that your company has two regional offices, East and West. Both offices use invoice numbers with six characters. Invoices generated by the East office consist of four digits followed by AA, and those generated by the West office consist of six digits that end with 00 (two zeros). Follow the steps below to see how Quattro Pro treats these invoice numbers:

Distributing labels

Quattro Pro has a command that enables you to break up long, multiword labels so that they fit within a column without flowing over into the next column. The resulting labels appear as if they are one label in paragraph form. Just select the cell with the long label, and choose Reformat from the Block menu. When you click OK, Quattro Pro breaks the label into chunks that fit in the existing column width, inserting as many cells as needed and moving down any existing entries. For example, the label *Now is the time for all good men to come to the aid of their country* is distributed into about seven standard-width cells, depending on font size. To reverse this action (when Undo Reformat is no longer possible), select the block of distributed labels, and drag to the right until the label fits horizontally in the selected block. Then choose Reformat again, and click OK. Quattro Pro does not delete the cells it inserted during the original Reformat operation, so you may have to make manual adjustments.

1. Click cell B2 to select it, type *4739AA*, and press Down Arrow. This invoice number consists of both digits and letters, so Quattro Pro displays an *Invalid reference* error message.

2. Click OK to close the message box. Quattro Pro places the insertion point at the beginning of the entry in the input line.

3. Type an apostrophe ('), and press Down Arrow. Quattro Pro now accepts the entry as a label.

4. In cell B3, which is now active, type *943200*, and click the ✓ button. This invoice number consists of only digits, so Quattro Pro treats the entry as a numeric value and right-aligns it in its cell.

5. To tell Quattro Pro to treat the entry as text, press F2 to activate the input line, click at the beginning of the entry, type an apostrophe, and press Enter. (Pressing Enter is the same as clicking the ✓ button.) Quattro Pro then overwrites the numeric value with the label and left-aligns the entry in its cell.

6. Enter these invoice numbers in the indicated cells, being sure to type the label-prefix character before all entries:

B4	'8488AA
B5	'4398AA
B6	'4945AA
B7	'825600
B8	'846500
B9	'4409AA
B10	'8867AA

Label-prefix characters

Instead of the apostrophe, which left-aligns labels, you can use a caret (^) to center labels or quotation marks (") to right-align them. To start a label with one of these characters, precede it with another label-prefix character.

Labels only

Quattro Pro considers any entry that starts with a digit or these characters:

/ + – $ (@ : #

to be a numeric entry. Instead of typing a label-prefix character before all numeric entries you want to use as labels, Quattro Pro provides an easier alternative. Just select the block in which the entries will be made, and click the block with the right mouse button to display the block Object Inspector. Choose the Data Entry Input property, and select Labels Only. To allow the block to accept numeric values, you will have to return to the block's Object Inspector and select the General option in the Data Entry Input property.

B11   '875600
B12   '479300

Your notebook page now looks like this:

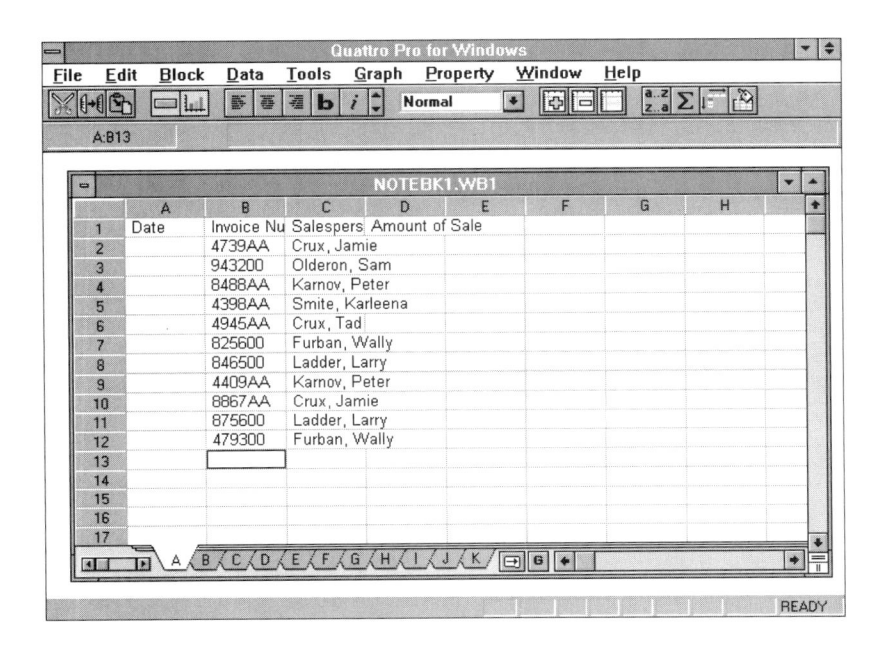

Entering Numeric Values

As you have seen, entering numeric values is just as easy as entering labels. Follow along with the next few steps, as we enter the sales amounts in column D:

1. Click cell D2 to select the first cell in the Amount of Sale column, type *83456.23*, and press Down Arrow. Quattro Pro records the entry and right-aligns it.

2. Enter the following amounts in the indicated cells, pressing the Down Arrow key after each one:

    D3   90875.56
    D4   634568.30
    D5   42356.07
    D6   65643.90
    D7   123456.50
    D8   67345.23
    D9   145768.34
    D10   43256.23
    D11   11256.90
    D12   85345.00

Don't worry if Quattro Pro doesn't display these values exactly as you entered them (see the tip below). On page 27, we format these amounts so that they display as dollars and cents.

Entering Dates and Times

Even seasoned Quattro Pro users sometimes have difficulty entering dates and times in their notebooks. For dates and times to be displayed correctly, you must first let Quattro Pro know that you are entering a date or time, by pressing Ctrl-Shift-D to turn on DATE mode. The DATE indicator then appears in the status line, and you can make entries in any of the following recognized formats:

Turning on DATE mode

09-Mar-92	09:15:30 AM
09-Mar	09:15 AM
Mar-92	09:15:30
03/09/92	09:15
03/09	

Let's get a feel for how Quattro Pro handles different date formats:

1. Enter the following dates in the indicated cells, pressing Ctrl-Shift-D before and Down Arrow after typing each one:

A2	03-Mar-92
A3	01/04/92
A4	10-Jan-92
A5	16-Jan-92

Long numeric values

As you have seen, Quattro Pro allows a long text entry to overflow into an adjacent empty cell and truncates the entry only if the adjacent cell also contains an entry. However, the program treats a long numeric value differently. If Quattro Pro displays asterisks (*) instead of the value you entered, the value is too large to display in the cell, and you must make the column wider to view it. Long non-dollar values are displayed in scientific notation, and values with many decimal places are rounded. For example, if you enter 12345678912345 in a standard-width cell (which is 9 characters wide), Quattro Pro displays 1.2E+13 (1.2 times 10 to the 13th power). If you enter 123456.789 in a standard-width cell, Quattro Pro displays 123456.8. In both cases, Quattro Pro leaves the underlying value unchanged. You can widen the column to display long numeric values the way you entered them. (Adjusting the width of columns is discussed on page 28.)

Chapter 1 Building a Simple Notebook

A6	03-Feb-92
A7	02/08/92
A8	02/14/92
A9	03/02/92
A10	03/12/92
A11	23-Mar-92
A12	30-Mar-92

If the date won't fit in the cell Quattro Pro fills the cell with a string of asterisks. Later, we'll come back and clean up the Date column so that the dates all appear in one format.

2. Now select cell A3. Quattro Pro displays a number in the input line. Although Quattro Pro displays dates and times in recognizable formats, it stores them as numbers that it can use in formulas.

As you can see, you have now completed all the columns of this simple notebook page.

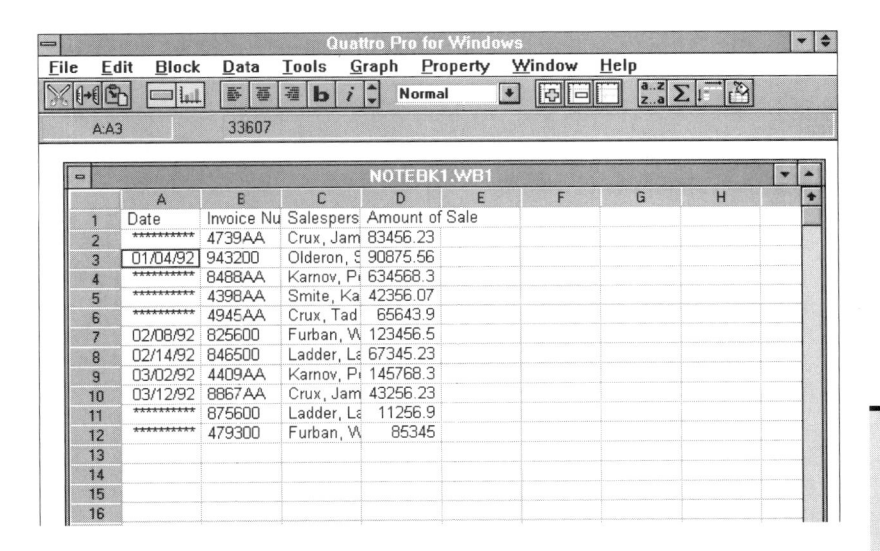

Selecting Blocks

Well, we've created a basic notebook. But before we can show you some of the things you can do with it, we need to discuss how to select groups of cells, called blocks. Any rectangular group of more than one cell is a block. A block can include two cells, an entire row or column, or an entire notebook page. Knowing how to select and work with blocks saves you time because you can apply formats to or reference

Entering dates

A quick way to format a block to accept dates without you having to press Ctrl-Shift-D for each cell is to select the block, and click it with the right mouse button to open the block Object Inspector. Then choose the Data Entry Input property, select Dates Only, and click OK.

the whole block, instead of having to deal with its component cells individually.

Block addresses

Blocks are referred to by the addresses of the cell in the top-left corner of the block and the cell in the bottom-right corner, separated by two periods. For example, A1..B2 identifies the block that consists of cells A1, A2, B1, and B2.

The simplest way to learn how to select blocks is to actually do it, so follow along as we demonstrate selecting blocks of different shapes and sizes.

1. Point to cell A1, hold down the left mouse button, and drag diagonally to cell D12 without releasing the button.

2. Release the mouse button. The block A1..D12 remains highlighted to indicate that it is selected. Cell A1—the cell where you started the selection—is white, to indicate that it is the active cell in the block. The address in the cell indicator, A:A1, indicates that cell A1 on notebook page A is active.

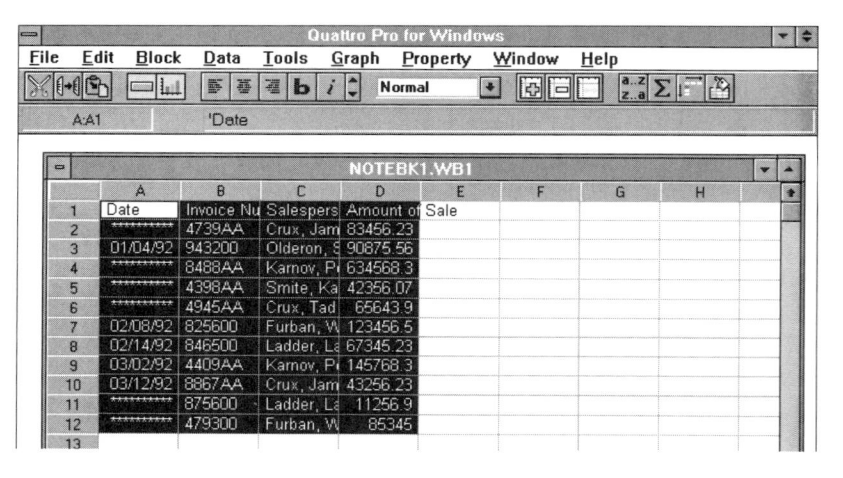

Selecting columns

3. Move the mouse pointer to the border of column B, and click the letter B. Quattro Pro simultaneously deselects A1..D12 and selects all of column B—the block B1..B8192.

4. Now point to the border of column C, hold down the mouse button, and drag through the border of column D. Two entire columns—the block C1..D8192—are selected.

5. Move the pointer to the border of row 6, and click the number 6 to select the entire row—the block A6..IV6.

6. Next, try selecting blocks with the keyboard. Select cell B6, hold down the Shift key, press the Right Arrow key twice and the Down Arrow key twice, and release the Shift key. The block B6..D8 is selected.

Selecting with the keyboard

The blocks you just selected were all sets of contiguous cells, but blocks can contain more than one set of cells. These blocks are referred to as discontiguous blocks. Try this:

1. Use any method to select the block A1..B2.

2. Hold down the Ctrl key, and use the mouse to select the block C4..D5. Your notebook now looks like this:

Selecting discontiguous blocks

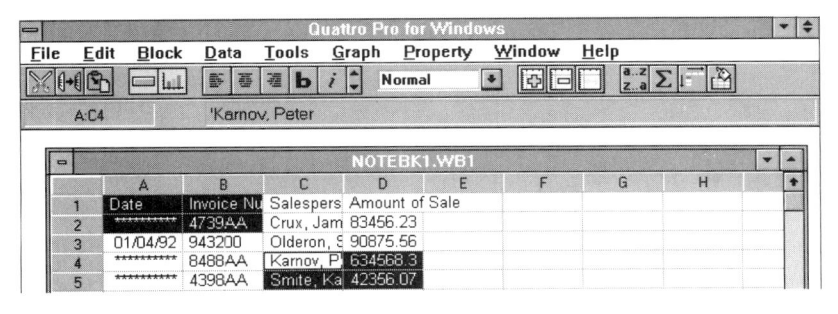

Notice that cell C4, the first cell of the second part of the block, is now the active cell.

Giving Quattro Pro Instructions

Now that you know how to select cells and blocks, let's quickly cover how you tell Quattro Pro what to do with your selection. You usually give Quattro Pro instructions by means of commands that are arranged in menus on the menu bar. Because this procedure is the same for all Windows applications, we assume that you are familiar with it, and we provide only a quick review here. If you are a new Windows user, we suggest that you spend a little time familiarizing yourself with the mechanics of menus, commands, and dialog boxes before proceeding.

To choose a command from a menu, you first click the name of the menu in the menu bar. When the menu drops down, you simply click the name of the command you want. From the keyboard, you can press Alt or the forward slash key (/) to activate the menu bar, press the underlined letter of the

Goto selection shortcut

A quick way to select a large block without using the mouse is to choose the Goto command from the Edit menu and enter the block reference in the Reference edit field. When you click OK, Quattro Pro scrolls to the block and selects it. To select a block on another notebook page, precede the block address with the page letter or name followed by a colon.

name of the menu, and then press the underlined letter of the command you want. Press Esc to reverse the process.

Unavailable commands

Some command names are displayed in "gray" letters, indicating that you can't choose those commands at this time, and some command names have an arrowhead next to them, indicating that choosing the command will cause a submenu to appear. You choose a submenu command just as you choose a regular command, using the mouse or the keyboard.

Submenus

Dialog boxes

Some command names are followed by an ellipsis (...), indicating that you must supply more information in a dialog box before Quattro Pro can carry out the command. You give the necessary information by typing in an edit field or by selecting options from list boxes, drop-down list boxes, or groups of check boxes and option buttons. Clicking one of the command buttons—usually OK—closes the dialog box and carries out the command according to your specifications. Clicking Cancel or Close, or pressing Esc, closes the dialog box and cancels the command. Other command buttons might be available to refine the original command or to open other dialog boxes with more options. Many dialog boxes also contain a Help button, which you use to get information about the dialog box.

Object Inspectors

Object Inspectors are context-sensitive menus and dialog boxes that group together frequently used formatting commands. Object Inspectors appear when you click an object—for example, a cell, a block, a notebook page tab, or a graph element—using the right mouse button. From now on, we will refer to this action as right-clicking.

The SpeedBar

Quattro Pro's SpeedBar is context-sensitive, which means that the SpeedBar changes depending on the type of window displayed. The SpeedBar also changes to reflect the actions you perform in a window. For example, when you make an entry in a notebook, the fourth and fifth SpeedBar buttons change to @ and { }, which you use when entering formulas.

You can display a second SpeedBar below the default one to carry out more tasks with a click of the mouse. Here's how:

Keyboard shortcuts

If you and your mouse don't get along and you prefer to use the keyboard, you can access many Quattro Pro commands by means of keyboard shortcuts. The list of shortcuts is extensive, and it would take a lot of space to reproduce it here. You can display the list by choosing the Keyboard command from the Help menu and then selecting a category from the Keyboard Techniques list.

Chapter 1 Building a Simple Notebook

1. Right-click the Quattro Pro for Windows title bar (not the notebook title bar) to display the application Object Inspector.

2. Click SpeedBar, and then click the Browse button to see the SpeedBars you can display below the default SpeedBar.

3. Click SECOND.BAR, and then click OK twice to return to the notebook window with a second SpeedBar displayed, as shown here:

Displaying a second SpeedBar

4. Move the pointer over each button in turn to display a brief description of its function at the left end of the status line.

In this book, we do not display the second SpeedBar, but you might want to spend some time experimenting with the available second SpeedBar options. If you want your screen to look like our illustrations, turn off the second SpeedBar when you are finished exploring, by right-clicking the application title bar to display its Object Inspector, clicking SpeedBar, clicking Reset, and then clicking OK to return to the notebook window with only the default SpeedBar displayed.

Saving Notebooks

With that brief overview out of the way, let's turn our attention back to the notebook we have created and find out how to save it for future use. Follow these steps:

1. Choose either Save or Save As from the File menu to display the Save File dialog box so that you can name the notebook.

2. In the File Name edit field, NOTEBK1.WB1 is the suggested name of the file. Overwrite this suggestion by typing *sales*. There's no need to supply an extension because Quattro Pro automatically adds the extension WB1 to indicate that the file is a Quattro Pro notebook.

3. Leave the other settings in the dialog box as they are for now, and click OK to carry out the command.

Custom SpeedBar

After you become familiar with the tools on the SpeedBar, you might want to customize it to include only the tools you use most often. Refer to the *Building Spreadsheet Applications* documentation to see how to create your own SpeedBar.

When you return to the Quattro Pro window, notice that the name SALES.WB1 has replaced NOTEBK1.WB1 in the notebook's title bar.

Saving existing notebooks

From now on, when you choose the Save command to save changes to this notebook, Quattro Pro does not display the Save File dialog box because it already knows the name of the notebook. Quattro Pro simply saves the notebook by overwriting the previous version with the new version.

Preserving previous versions

If you want to save the changes you have made to a notebook but preserve the previous version, you can assign the new version a different name by choosing the Save As command from the File menu, entering the new name in the File Name edit field, and clicking OK. If you click OK without entering a new name, Quattro Pro displays a warning message. You can click Replace to overwrite the existing notebook or Backup to change the extension of the existing notebook to BAK, thereby preserving the existing version and the new version.

Creating New Notebooks

Having saved the notebook, let's create a new one so that we can see how to work with more than one notebook at the same time. Follow these steps:

File-naming conventions

DOS file-naming conventions apply to Quattro Pro notebook names. The names you assign to notebooks must be eight or fewer characters and can include letters, numbers, and the following characters:

_ ^ $! # % & - { } ( )

They cannot contain spaces, commas, or periods.

Designating a directory

By default, notebooks are saved in the directory in which you installed Quattro Pro. To save to another directory, select that directory from the Directories list in the Save File dialog box before clicking OK. To change the default directory, right-click the Quattro Pro title bar to open the application Object Inspector, select the Startup property, and in the Directory edit field, enter the path of the new default directory.

Password protection

You can assign a password of up to 15 characters to a notebook. Choose Save As, enter a filename, and then enter the password in the Protection Password edit field. When you click OK, Quattro Pro asks you to type the password again to verify it. (Passwords are case sensitive.) Quattro Pro then requires that the password be entered correctly before it will open the notebook.

1. Choose New from the File menu. Quattro Pro opens a new blank notebook with the name NOTEBK2.WB1, overlapping SALES.WB1. Your screen looks like this:

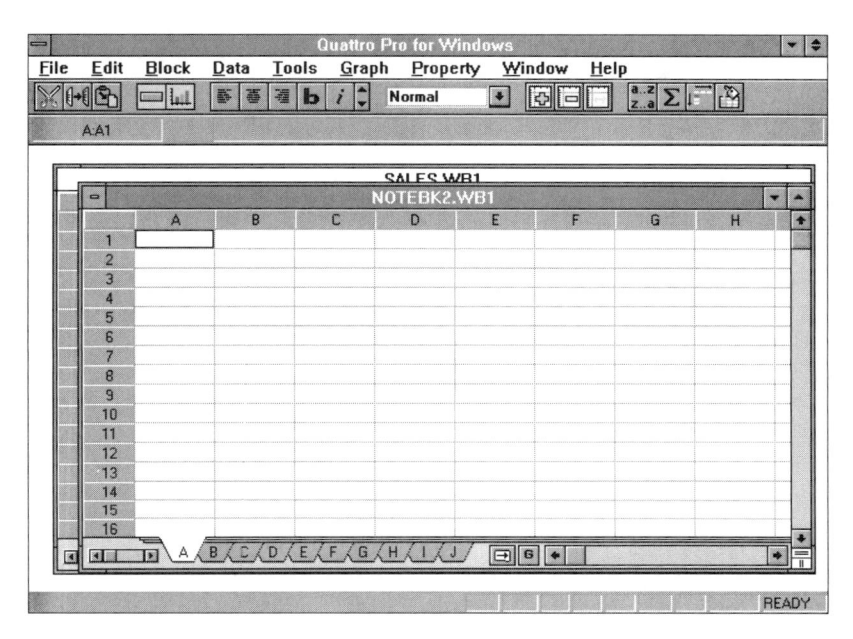

That's all there is to it. You now have two notebooks open on your screen with which to experiment.

Manipulating Windows

Let's take a moment to review some window basics. Being able to work with more than one notebook open at a time is useful, especially if you frequently need to use the same set of numbers in different notebooks. For example, you might use the same raw data to develop a budget, work out a trial balance, or create an income statement. Follow these steps to see how easy it is to move among notebooks:

1. Click any visible part of SALES.WB1 to make it the active notebook. If you can't see SALES.WB1, choose it from the list of open notebooks at the bottom of the Window menu. Notice that the color of its title bar changes to indicate that it is the active notebook.

2. Now choose Tile from the Window menu. Quattro Pro arranges the two notebooks so that they each occupy half the screen, as shown on the next page.

Arranging windows

Maximizing windows

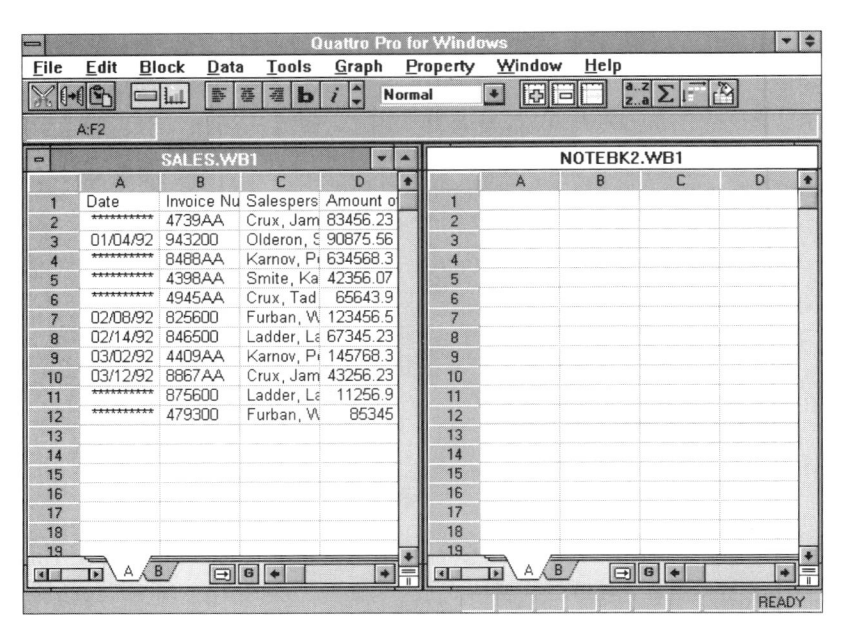

3. Click anywhere in NOTEBK2.WB1 to make it the active notebook.

4. Click the Maximize button (the upward-pointing arrow at the right end of NOTEBK2.WB1's title bar—not the application's title bar). NOTEBK2.WB1 expands to fill the screen, completely obscuring SALES.WB1.

5. Pull down the Window menu. Again, the names of the two open notebooks appear at the bottom of the menu, with a check mark indicating the active one.

Hiding windows

Use the Hide command on the Window menu to hide the active window. For example, you might want to hide one or more of the open windows before choosing the Tile or Cascade command. If the hidden notebook contains macros, all macros in the notebook are active even though the notebook is not visible. To make a window reappear, choose the Show command, select the window, and click OK.

Minimizing to icons

Just as you can minimize group windows to icons in Program Manager, you can minimize notebook windows to icons in Quattro Pro. In this way, you can keep many notebooks open at the same time without cluttering up the screen or obscuring other notebooks.

One notebook, two views

To view different parts of the same notebook, activate the notebook, and choose New View from the Window menu. Quattro Pro opens another window for the notebook and appends :2 to the filename in the window's title bar. You can then use the Tile command to arrange the windows and use the scroll bars to view different cells and pages of the notebook at the same time.

6. Choose SALES.WB1 from the Window menu. The two notebooks switch places, and SALES.WB1 now completely obscures NOTEBK2.WB1. (When you maximize one window, all of the windows in the "stack" of windows become maximized.)

Editing Basics

In this section, we briefly cover some simple ways of revising and manipulating notebooks so that in subsequent chapters we can give general editing instructions without having to go into great detail.

Changing Entries

First, let's see how to change individual entries. Glancing at the Amount of Sale column in SALES.WB1, notice that the amount in cell D4 is suspiciously large compared with all the other amounts. Suppose you check this number and find to your disappointment that the amount should be 63456.83, not 634568.3. Here's how you make the correction without having to retype the entire number:

1. Select cell D4.

2. Click the input line, or press F2 to activate it.

3. Move the pointer to the input line between the 6 and the 8, and click the mouse button. Quattro Pro places a blinking insertion point between the two numbers, and the mode indicator in the status line changes to EDIT.

4. Type a period (.), and press Right Arrow.

5. Press the Del (or Delete) key to delete the second period.

6. Press Enter to record the corrected entry in the cell.

Copying Entries

You can copy an entry or group of entries anywhere within the same notebook or to a different notebook. Copy operations involve the use of two commands: Copy and Paste (or their button equivalents). Follow the steps on the next page.

> **Scroll bars**
>
> Using the scroll bars to bring cells into view does not change the active cell. As a result, you can pause in the middle of making an entry to view a cell in a different area of the notebook and then return to the active cell with your incomplete entry still in the input line, just as you left it.

1. Select A1..D12, and click the Copy button on the SpeedBar.

2. Select cell E1, and click the Paste button on the SpeedBar. Notice that you do not have to select a block of cells in which to paste the copied block. Quattro Pro assumes that the selected cell is the location of the top-left corner of the paste area.

3. Select cell F1, and choose Paste from the Edit menu. Again, Quattro Pro uses the selected cell as the top-left corner of the paste area and, without warning, pastes the entries over the existing contents of cells F1..I12.

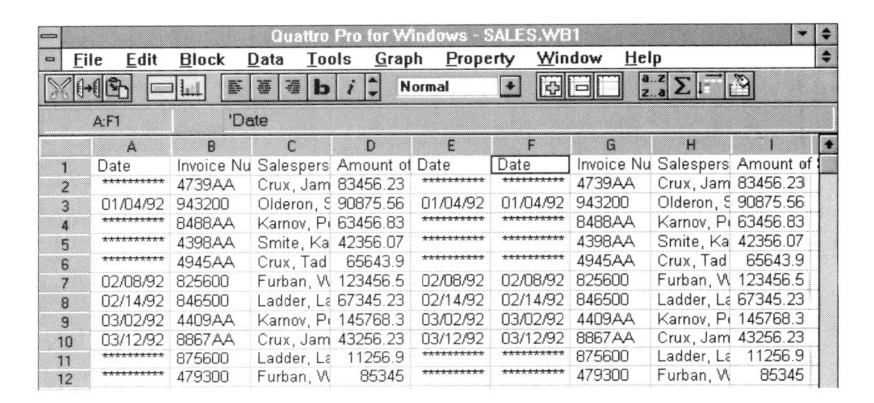

Cause for panic? Not at all. Quattro Pro's Undo command is designed for just such an occasion. (Undo must be enabled. See the tip below.)

Undoing commands

4. Choose Undo Paste from the Edit menu. Quattro Pro restores your notebook to its prepaste status.

Keyboard shortcuts

You can use the keyboard to move around the notebook. You'll use the Arrow keys most often, but as you gain more experience with Quattro Pro you might find other keys useful. (Note that navigating with the keyboard always relocates the active cell.) Here's a list of navigation keys and what they do:

Key	Action
PgDn	Moves down one screen
PgUp	Moves up one screen
Ctrl-PgDn	Moves forward one page
Ctrl-PgUp	Moves backward one page
Home	Moves to cell A1 of the current notebook page
Ctrl-Home	Moves to cell A1 of page A
End-Home	Moves to the lower-right corner of the nonblank part of the notebook page
Ctrl-Right Arrow or **Tab**	Moves right one screen
Ctrl-Left Arrow or **Shift-Tab**	Moves left one screen
F5 (Goto)	Moves to the cell or block you specify

Quattro Pro provides another way to cut, copy, and paste entries within a notebook using a simple mouse operation called Drag and Drop. You can use Drag and Drop as long as you have more than one cell selected.

Copying with Drag and Drop

1. Reselect A1..D12, and then move the pointer within the selected block. Press the Ctrl key, and hold down the mouse button. The pointer changes to a small "grabbing hand."

2. Drag an outline of the selection over block E1..H12.

3. Release the mouse button and the Ctrl key. Quattro Pro asks *Overwrite non-blank cells in destination block?*

4. Click Yes. Quattro Pro pastes a copy of the selected block into E1..H12 and highlights the copy.

The result of this operation is nearly identical to using the Copy and Paste commands. However, because Quattro Pro doesn't place a copy of the selected block on the Clipboard, you can use this technique to copy and paste the selected block only once within a single notebook page. Because Drag and Drop requires that you hold down the mouse button and drag the copy to the destination block, it's also probably best reserved for copying and pasting small blocks a short distance from the original.

Follow the steps on the next page to make yet another copy, this time in NOTEBK2.WB1.

The Clipboard

The Windows Clipboard is a temporary storage space used to hold cut or copied data from all Windows applications. You can use it to transfer data within one notebook, between notebooks, or between applications.

Temporary storage

Because the Windows Clipboard is a temporary storage space, exiting Windows or turning off your computer erases any information that is stored there, unless you save the Clipboard file. Save the file by switching to Program Manager, double-clicking the Clipboard (or Clipboard Viewer) icon to display the Clipboard window, and choosing Save As from the File menu.

Clipboard contents

If you cut or copy cells and then double-click the Clipboard (or Clipboard Viewer) icon in Program Manager, instead of displaying a copy of the cells and their contents, the Clipboard indicates the cut or copied block location and size. For example, *D:B12..C34* indicates that block B12..C34 on page D was cut or copied. This display has no effect on the result of pasting the cut or copied cells.

1. Choose NOTEBK2.WB1 from the bottom of the Window menu, and check that cell A1 is active.

2. Choose Paste from the Edit menu or click the Paste button on the SpeedBar. Quattro Pro faithfully pastes in a copy of the block from SALES.WB1. You can use the same technique to copy and paste blocks between notebook pages.

Moving Entries

The procedure for moving entries is similar to that for copying entries. In this case, you use two commands: Cut and Paste. Try this:

1. Choose the Tile command from the Window menu to display both open notebooks.

2. Activate SALES.WB1, and use the bottom scroll bar to move columns E through H into view.

3. Select E1..H12 in SALES.WB1, and choose Cut from the Edit menu or click the Cut button on the SpeedBar. The cell entries disappear from the block.

4. Select cell A13 in NOTEBK2.WB1. Then either choose Paste from the Edit menu or click the Paste button. Quattro Pro inserts the entries from E1..H12 of SALES.WB1 in A13..D24 of NOTEBK2.WB1. Your notebooks now look like this:

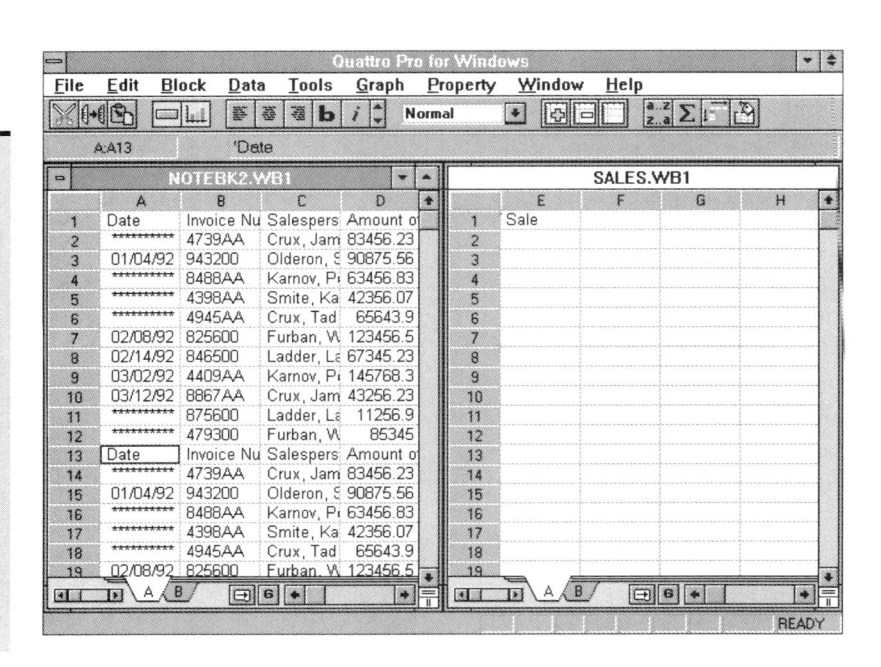

Using Undo

The examples in this book require that the Undo function be enabled. Right-click the Quattro Pro title bar to display the application Object Inspector. Choose the Startup property, and in the Options list, check that Undo Enabled is selected. If it isn't, select it, and click OK.

5. To get a better view of the results in SALES.WB1, activate the window, click its Maximize button, and press Home to bring cell A1 into view.

You can also use Drag and Drop editing to move a block within a single notebook. Try this:

Moving with Drag and Drop

1. Select A1..D12, move the pointer within the block, and hold down the mouse button.

2. Drag the block to a new location in the notebook, and release the mouse button. If the destination block has no cell entries, the selected block simply moves to its new location. If any of the cells in the destination block contain entries, Quattro Pro asks *Overwrite non-blank cells in destination block?* Click Yes to overwrite the cells, or click No to undo the Drag and Drop operation.

3. Choose Undo Block Move from the Edit menu to undo this editing action.

Clearing Cells

Let's tidy up NOTEBK2.WB1 by getting rid of the extraneous copies of your data. You want to erase the entries in cells A1..D24—in Quattro Pro jargon, you want to *clear the cells*. Clearing cells is different from cutting entries. Cutting entries assumes that you will paste the entries somewhere else, whereas clearing cells simply erases the entries. To clear cells, try the following steps.

Copying vs. moving

Remember, if you want to copy a block of cells using Drag and Drop editing, hold down the Ctrl key while dragging the mouse. If you want to move the cells, simply drag, without holding down an additional key.

Block commands

In addition to using the Cut, Copy, and Paste commands, the similarly named buttons on the Speedbar, and Drag and Drop, you can use two commands on the Block menu—Move and Copy—to carry out these actions. Use these commands to move and copy blocks long distances and to move and copy blocks to other notebook pages. To copy a block, first select it, and then choose Copy from the Block menu. In the To edit field in the Block Copy dialog box, enter the address of the destination block, and click OK. Follow the same steps to move a block, but choose Move instead of Copy.

1. Choose NOTEBK2.WB1 from the Window menu, and select cells A1..D24 (drag down beyond the window to scroll row 24 into view).

2. Choose Clear from the Edit menu. Quattro Pro clears the entries and any formatting from the selected cells.

3. Press Home, and the notebook now looks as it did before you started pasting entries into it.

Inserting and Deleting Cells

It is a rare person who can create a notebook from scratch without ever having to tinker with its design—moving this block of data, changing that label, or adding or deleting a column here and there. In this section, we'll show you how to insert and delete cells. Follow these steps:

1. Choose SALES.WB1 from the Window menu to activate it.

Inserting columns

2. Click the border of column D to select the entire column.

3. Choose Insert from the Block menu, and then choose Columns from the Insert submenu. Quattro Pro inserts an entire blank column in front of the Amount of Sale column which, as you can see here, is now column E:

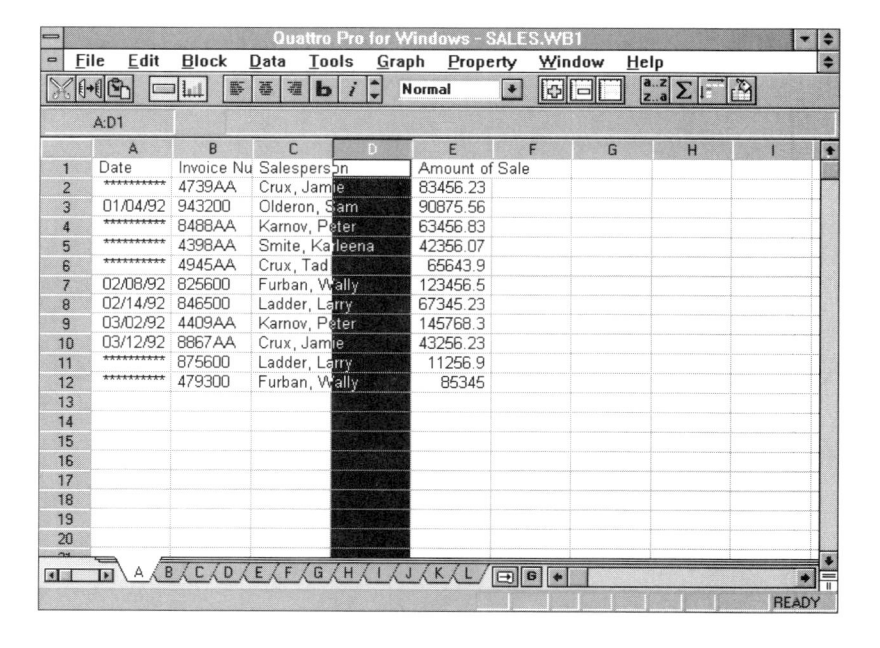

Inserting a row works the same way as inserting a column. You simply click the row border and choose Rows from the Insert submenu.

Inserting rows

Another way to insert rows and columns is to click the Insert button on the SpeedBar, like this:

1. Choose Undo Block Insert from the Edit menu.

2. With column D selected, click the Insert button. Quattro Pro reinserts the blank column.

What if you need to insert only a few cells and inserting an entire column will mess up some of your entries? You can insert cells anywhere you need them, as you'll see if you follow these steps:

1. Select E1..E10—all but two of the cells containing entries in column E—and click the Insert button. Quattro Pro displays this dialog box:

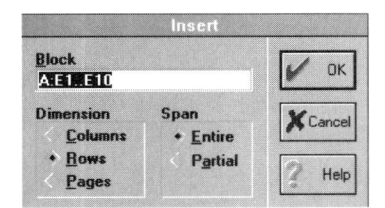

Because you have selected a block rather than the entire column, Quattro Pro needs to know which cells to move to make room for the inserted cells.

2. Select the Columns and Partial options, and then click OK. Quattro Pro inserts a new blank cell to the left of each selected cell, as shown on the next page.

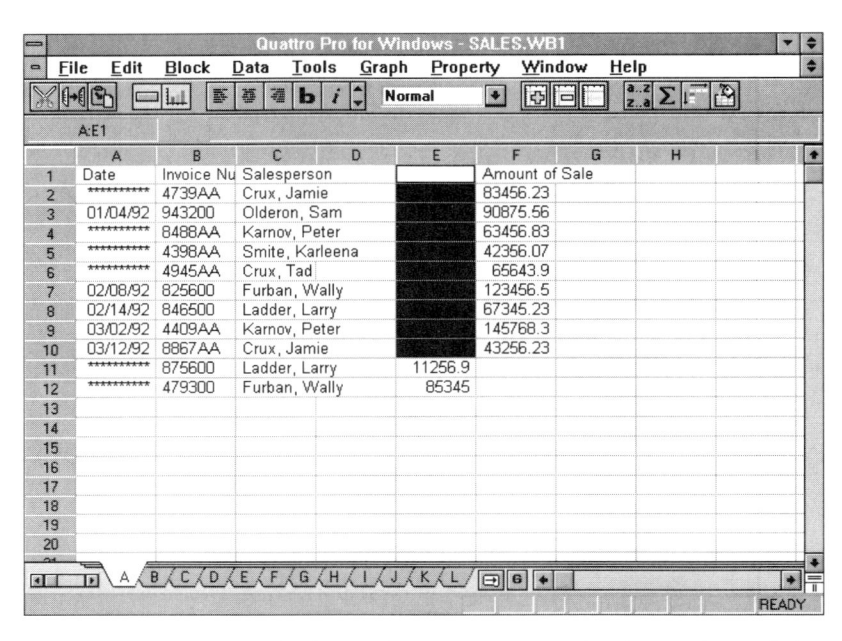

You could undo this insertion to restore the integrity of the Amount of Sale column, but instead let's delete E1..E10:

1. With E1..E10 selected, click the Delete button on the SpeedBar. Quattro Pro displays a Delete dialog box similar to the Insert dialog box to find out how to close up the space that will be left by the deleted cells.

2. Select Columns and Partial again, and then click OK. Quattro Pro deletes the cells, and the sales amounts are now back in one column.

Formatting Basics

Quattro Pro offers a wide variety of formatting options that allow you to emphasize parts of your notebooks and display data in different ways. Here we'll use one of the buttons on the SpeedBar, and we'll explore the formatting options available through the block Object Inspector.

Changing Notebook Formatting

Just as you can use labels to make tables of data easier to read, you can use formatting to distinguish different categories of information. You could spend a lot of time manually formatting a table to get it to look perfect. Fortunately, Quattro Pro provides some buttons that make formatting a snap.

1. Select the block A1..E12.

2. Click the SpeedFormat button on the SpeedBar to display this dialog box, in which Quattro Pro lists several different automatic formatting options:

Using SpeedFormat

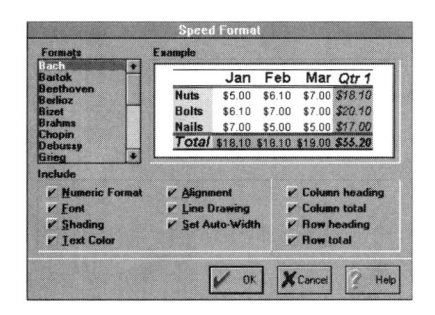

3. For now, accept the default choice in the Formats list, deselect the Column Total and Row Heading options, and click OK. Quattro Pro instantly formats the block as shown here:

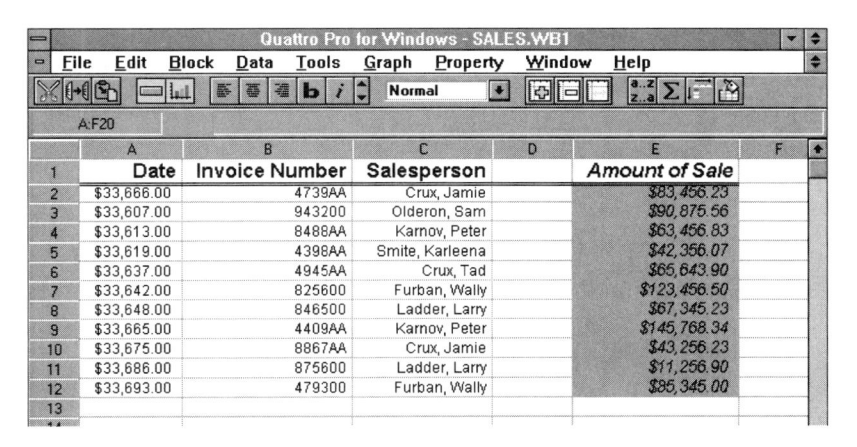

Quattro Pro made the text at the top of the columns larger and bold-faced, made the columns wide enough to display the entire cell entries, and added a border below the labels to set them off. (If you click one of the cells containing labels, you will see that the Bold button on the SpeedBar appears "pressed," indicating that this format is in effect for the selected cell.) Quattro Pro also shaded the cells in the Amount of Sale column and italicized these entries. Making all these changes manually would have meant using buttons on the SpeedBar or changing the Font, Shading, Alignment, Line Drawing, and Column Width properties in the Object Inspectors of specific blocks of cells.

SpeedFormat options

The SpeedFormat dialog box has over 20 colorful table types to choose from. To see what they look like, select a type, and look at the sample table in the Example box. Then select or deselect options in the Include box, and watch the sample table change. Click OK when you're satisfied with the formatting.

You may also have noticed that Quattro Pro now displays the dates as dollar values: To give the dates a uniform date format, follow these steps:

1. Select the block A2..A12, and then right-click the block. Quattro Pro displays the Object Inspector for the active block:

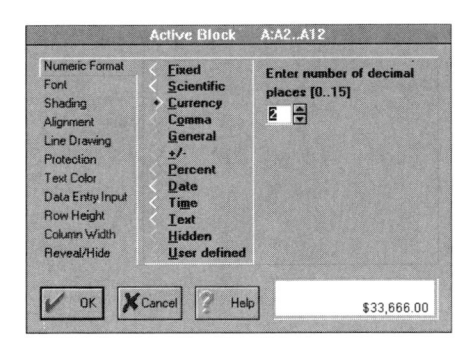

By selecting the different properties on the left side of the Object Inspector and then selecting options on the right side, you can change dozens of aspects of block formatting. (Although you can cut or copy formatting along with cell entries, it is the cells that are actually formatted, not the entries.) The options available for the Numeric Format property are currently displayed.

Formatting dates

2. Click Date in the middle list, and select Long Date Intl. in the list on the right.

3. Click OK. Quattro Pro reformats the date values so that they are displayed as dates instead of currency. The dates are now formatted uniformly.

Changing Column Widths

When you are manually formatting cells, cell entries may occasionally overflow into neighboring cells because of the formatting. For example, suppose some of the salespeople's names in column C ran over into column D. You can use several techniques to widen column C to display the names properly.

1. For this example, enter *Ferdinand, Aloysius* in cell C13. The name runs over into column D, as you can see here:

Chapter 1 Building a Simple Notebook

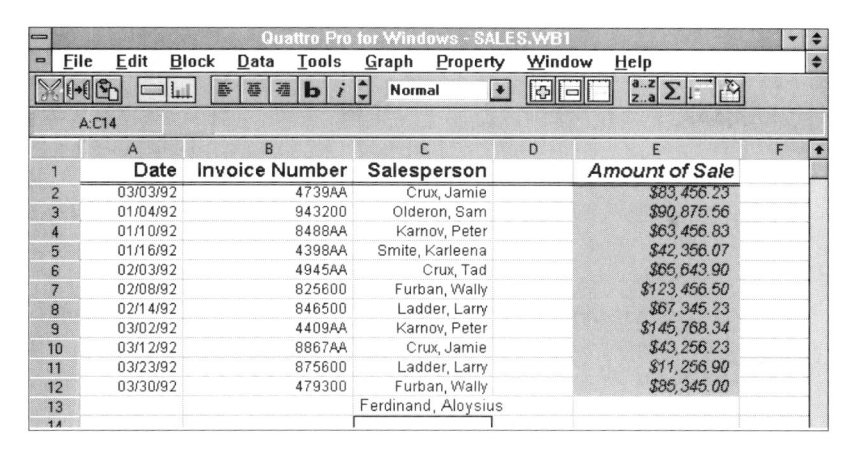

	A	B	C	D	E	F
1	Date	Invoice Number	Salesperson		Amount of Sale	
2	03/03/92	4739AA	Crux, Jamie		$83,456.23	
3	01/04/92	943200	Olderon, Sam		$90,875.56	
4	01/10/92	8488AA	Karnov, Peter		$63,456.83	
5	01/16/92	4398AA	Smite, Karleena		$42,356.07	
6	02/03/92	4945AA	Crux, Tad		$65,643.90	
7	02/08/92	825600	Furban, Wally		$123,456.50	
8	02/14/92	846500	Ladder, Larry		$67,345.23	
9	03/02/92	4409AA	Karnov, Peter		$145,768.34	
10	03/12/92	8867AA	Crux, Jamie		$43,256.23	
11	03/23/92	875600	Ladder, Larry		$11,256.90	
12	03/30/92	479300	Furban, Wally		$85,345.00	
13			Ferdinand, Aloysius			

2. Move the mouse pointer to the dividing line between the column C border and the column D border. The pointer shape changes to a vertical bar with two opposing arrows.

    Manual adjustment

3. Hold down the mouse button, and drag to the right until column C is wide enough to display the name in C13. Release the mouse button when you think that the text will fit in the cell.

Now try another method:

1. First, choose Undo Column Sizing from the Edit menu. Quattro Pro returns the column to its original size.

2. Select any cell in column C, and click the Fit button on the SpeedBar. Quattro Pro automatically makes the entire column wide enough to contain the longest entry in the column.

    Automatic adjustment

The Auto Width option

To adjust a column's width so that all its entries are visible, right-click any cell in the column to display the block Object Inspector. Next select the Column Width property, then select the Auto Width option, and click OK.

The default width

To return a column to its default width, open the block Object Inspector by right-clicking any cell in the column, and then select Reset Width in the Column Width property. The default width is determined by the page Object Inspector. Right-click the page tab, and then set a new width in the Column Width edit field in the Default Width property.

Adjusting row height

You can adjust the height of rows the same way you adjust the width of columns. Simply drag the bottom line of the row border up or down, or set the height by selecting the Row Height property of the block Object Inspector.

1. Choose Undo Property Set from the Edit menu.
2. Clear the entry from cell C13.

Getting Help

This tour of Quattro Pro has covered a lot of ground in a few pages, and you might be wondering how you will manage to retain it all. Don't worry. If you forget how to carry out a particular task, help is never far away. For example, let's see how you would remind yourself of how to save a notebook:

1. Use the keyboard to open the File menu, and highlight the Save command. (Press Alt-F, and then press Down Arrow three times.)

Context-sensitive help

2. Press F1. Instead of actually saving the notebook, Quattro Pro displays this Help screen:

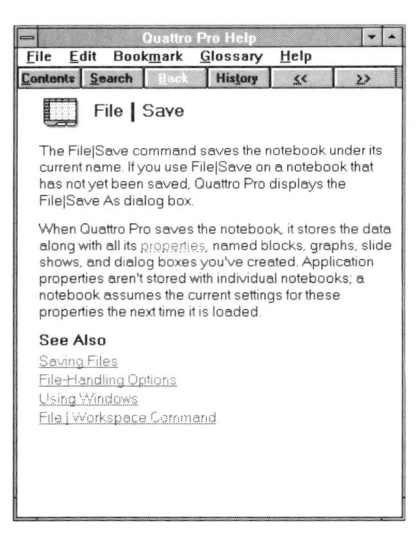

3. Click the Contents button to display a list of topics, which provide information on almost every aspect of Quattro Pro. (To get to this screen directly, press F1 in Quattro Pro without a dialog box or a menu open. If you press F1 in a dialog box, Quattro Pro provides context-sensitive help for that dialog box.)

4. Choose Exit from Help's File menu to return to your notebook window.

Quitting Quattro Pro

Well, that's it for the basic tour. All that's left is to show you how to end a Quattro Pro session. Follow these steps:

1. Choose Exit from the File menu.

2. When Quattro Pro asks whether to save the changes you have made to the open notebooks, click Yes and then Replace for SALES.WB1, and click No for NOTEBK2.WB1.

2
Analyzing Income

Opening Existing Notebooks 34
Simple Calculations 34
Doing Arithmetic 35
Totaling Columns of Values 36
Using the SpeedSum Button 36
Using the @SUM Function 37
Using References to Formula Cells in Other Formulas 38
Naming Cells and Blocks...39
Efficient Data Display..41
Creating a Calculation Area..41
More Formatting Techniques..43
Using Styles 45
More Calculations 48
Averaging Values...48
Identifying Highest and Lowest Sales 50
Calculating with Names 50
Formulas That Make Decisions 52
Using the @IF Function...52
Using Nested @IF Functions 53
Copying Formulas..54
Printing Notebooks 56
Print Preview...56
Setting Up the Pages 58
Getting Ready to Print...60

Opening notebooks
Page 34

Applying styles
Page 47

Changing fonts and sizes
Page 44

Quick addition
Page 37

Inserting rows
Page 35

Adding borders
Page 43

The @MAX function
Page 50

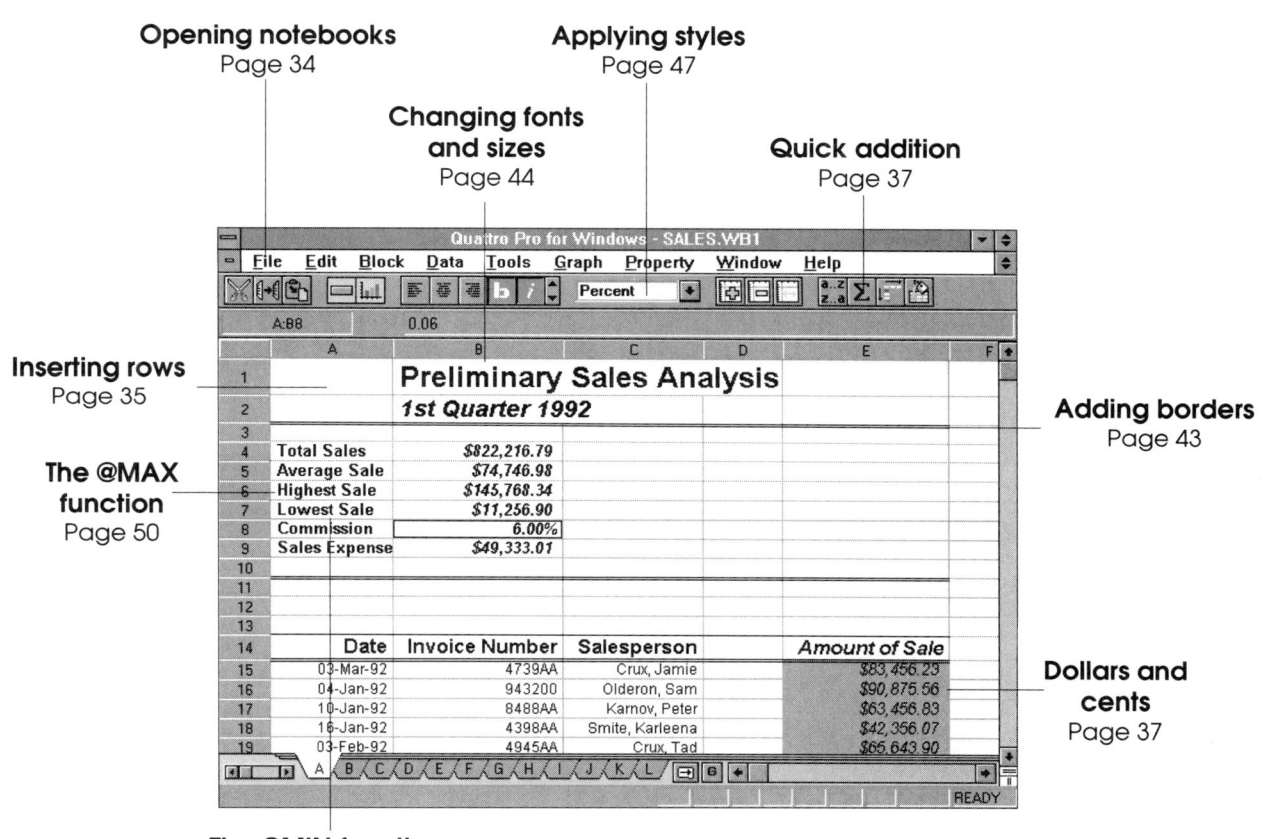

Dollars and cents
Page 37

The @MIN function
Page 50

Quattro Pro for Windows - SALES.WB1

File Edit Block Data Tools Graph Property Window Help

Percent

A:B8   0.06

	A	B	C	D	E
1		**Preliminary Sales Analysis**			
2		*1st Quarter 1992*			
3					
4	Total Sales	$822,216.79			
5	Average Sale	$74,746.98			
6	Highest Sale	$145,768.34			
7	Lowest Sale	$11,256.90			
8	Commission		6.00%		
9	Sales Expense	$49,333.01			
10					
11					
12					
13					
14	Date	Invoice Number	Salesperson		*Amount of Sale*
15	03-Mar-92	4739AA	Crux, Jamie		$83,456.23
16	04-Jan-92	943200	Olderon, Sam		$90,875.56
17	10-Jan-92	8488AA	Karnov, Peter		$63,456.83
18	16-Jan-92	4398AA	Smite, Karleena		$42,356.07
19	03-Feb-92	4945AA	Crux, Tad		$65,643.90

READY

Chapter 1 covered a lot of Quattro Pro basics, and you now know enough to create simple tables. However, you are missing the essential piece of information that turns a table into a notebook: how to enter formulas. The whole purpose of building notebooks is to have Quattro Pro perform calculations for you. In this chapter, we show you how to retrieve the SALES.WB1 notebook and enter formulas to analyze sales. (If you don't work in sales, you can adapt the notebook to analyze other sources of income, such as service fees.) Along the way, you learn some powerful techniques for manipulating your data, and we cover the principles of notebook design. Finally, we print the SALES.WB1 notebook. So fire up Quattro Pro, and we'll get started.

Opening Existing Notebooks

When you first start Quattro Pro, the notebook window contains a blank notebook entitled NOTEBK1.WB1. You can open a previously saved notebook using the Open command on the File menu, like this:

Closing notebooks

1. If a blank NOTEBK1.WB1 is displayed on your screen, conserve your computer's memory by closing it. Simply choose Close from the File menu.

Opening notebooks

2. Choose the Open command from the File menu, and locate and open SALES.WB1. Quattro Pro displays the table you created in Chapter 1.

3. If necessary, click the notebook's Maximize button to make the notebook as large as possible.

Simple Calculations

@Functions

Quattro Pro has many powerful @functions that are a sort of shorthand for the various formulas used in mathematical, statistical, financial, trigonometric, logical, logarithmic, and other types of calculations. However, the majority of notebooks created with Quattro Pro involve simple arithmetic. In this section, we show you how to use the four arithmetic operators (+, –, *, and /) to add, subtract, multiply, and divide, and then we introduce two Quattro Pro features with which you can quickly add sets of numeric values.

Doing Arithmetic

You must begin all formulas you enter in Excel with a digit from 0 through 9, or one of the following characters: . (a period), +, –, (, @, #, or $. Which number or character you use depends on what type of formula you are entering.

In the simplest formulas, you just type in the set of values separated by +, –, *, or /, such as

5+3+2

If you type this formula in any blank cell in your notebook and then press the Down Arrow key, Quattro Pro displays the result 10. You can also tell Quattro Pro to use the values in particular cells in its calculations, by entering their addresses in a formula. For example, the formula

+A3–A2

tells Quattro Pro to subtract the value in cell A2 from the value in cell A3. The plus sign indicates that the entry is a formula, not a label.

Let's experiment with a few formulas. We'll start by inserting a couple of blank rows:

1. Click the row 1 border, and drag down to the row 2 border to select the two rows.

2. Click the Insert button on the SpeedBar. Because you selected two rows, Quattro Pro inserts two blank rows above the table, moving the table down so that it begins in row 3.

Now we're ready to construct a formula in cell A1, using some of the values in the Amount of Sale column. We could retype these values in the input line to create the formula, but instead we'll tell Quattro Pro to use a value simply by clicking the cell that contains it. Follow these steps:

1. Click cell A1 to select it, and type a plus sign followed by an opening parenthesis.

2. Click cell E4. Quattro Pro inserts the cell reference E4 in the input line.

Inserting rows

Order of precedence

Unless you tell Quattro Pro to do otherwise, the program performs multiplication and division before addition and subtraction. If you want Quattro Pro to calculate part of a formula in a different order, enclose that part in parentheses. Quattro Pro then performs the calculations in parentheses before any other operations.

3. Type a plus sign, and click cell E5. Quattro Pro adds the cell reference E5 to the formula.

4. Continue to build the formula by typing plus signs and clicking cells E6, E7, and E8.

5. Type a closing parenthesis followed by a / (the division operator), and then type 5. The input line looks like this:

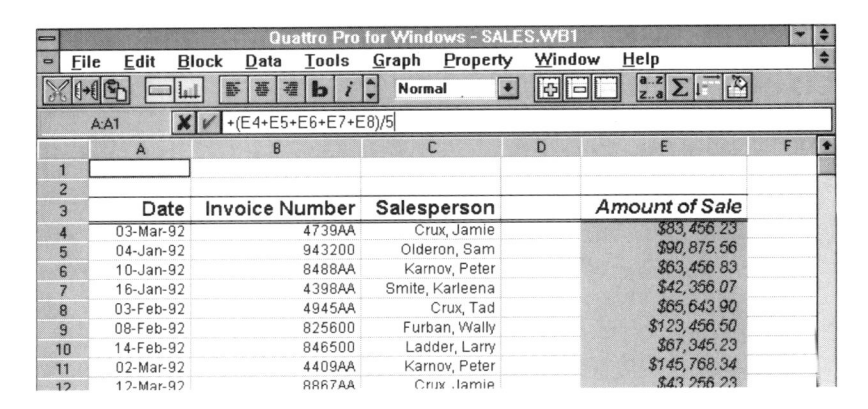

This formula tells Quattro Pro to first add the amounts in cells E4, E5, E6, E7, and E8 and then divide the result by 5, to obtain the average of the five amounts.

6. Click the ✓ button. Quattro Pro displays the result of the formula, 69157.718, in cell A1. Notice that the formula also remains in the input line.

You can use these techniques to create any simple formula. Just type an opening character (if necessary), and then type a value or click the cell that contains the value, type the appropriate arithmetic operator, enter the next value, and so on.

Displaying and editing formulas

By default, Quattro Pro displays the results of formulas in cells, not the underlying formulas. To see the actual underlying formulas in the notebook, select the cell and look at the input line. To edit the formula, first activate the input line by clicking it or pressing F2. Then click an insertion point and edit the formula as you would edit a label.

Totaling Columns of Values

Although this method of creating a formula is simple enough, it would be tedious to have to type and click to create long formulas. Fortunately, Quattro Pro automates the process of totaling a series of numeric values with a very useful button: the SpeedSum button on the SpeedBar.

Using the SpeedSum Button The SpeedSum button will probably become your most often used Quattro Pro button. Using this button is so easy that we'll dispense with explanations and simply show you how:

Chapter 2 Analyzing Income

1. Select E15, and then click the SpeedSum button. Quattro Pro looks above and to the left of the active cell for the largest block of numeric values to total. Because there are no values to the left of cell E15, Quattro Pro assumes that you want to total the values above it. Quattro Pro then enters an @SUM function in cell E15. (We discuss the @SUM function next.) Your notebook now looks like this:

	A	B	C	D	E
1	69157.718				
2					
3	Date	Invoice Number	Salesperson		Amount of Sale
4	03-Mar-92	4739AA	Crux, Jamie		$83,456.23
5	04-Jan-92	943200	Olderon, Sam		$90,875.56
6	10-Jan-92	8488AA	Karnov, Peter		$63,456.83
7	16-Jan-92	4398AA	Smite, Karleena		$42,356.07
8	03-Feb-92	4945AA	Crux, Tad		$65,643.90
9	08-Feb-92	825600	Furban, Wally		$123,456.50
10	14-Feb-92	846500	Ladder, Larry		$67,345.23
11	02-Mar-92	4409AA	Karnov, Peter		$145,768.34
12	12-Mar-92	8867AA	Crux, Jamie		$43,256.23
13	23-Mar-92	875600	Ladder, Larry		$11,256.90
14	30-Mar-92	479300	Furban, Wally		$85,345.00
15					822216.79

A:E15   @SUM(E3..E14)

Quattro Pro displays the result 822216.79—the sum of the values in E4..E14.

2. Format cell E15 as currency by right-clicking the cell to open its Object Inspector, selecting Currency as the Numeric Format property, checking that the number of decimal places is 2, and clicking OK.

Dollars and cents

Well, that was easy. The SpeedSum button will serve you well whenever you want a total to appear at the bottom of a column or to the right of a row of numeric values. But what if you want the total to appear elsewhere on the notebook? Knowing how to create @SUM functions from scratch gives you more flexibility.

Using the @SUM Function   Let's go back and dissect the @SUM function that Quattro Pro inserted in cell E15 when you clicked the SpeedSum button so that you can become familiar with the function's components. Clicking cell E15 puts this entry in the input line:

@SUM(E3..E14)

Function syntax

As its name implies, the @SUM function (and all @functions) begins with an "at" symbol. Next comes the function name in capital letters, followed by a set of parentheses enclosing the address of the block containing the amounts you want to total. This address is the @SUM function's argument. An argument answers questions such as "What?" or "How?" and gives Quattro Pro the additional information it needs to perform the function. In the case of @SUM, Quattro Pro needs only one piece of information—the addresses of the cells you want it to total. (Quattro Pro ignores any cells in the block that contain labels, as E3 does in this case.) As you'll see later in this chapter, Quattro Pro might need several pieces of information to carry out other @functions, and you enter an argument for each piece.

Creating an @SUM formula from scratch is not particularly difficult. To see how, follow these steps:

1. Select A1, and type this:

The @SUM function

@SUM(

When you select a cell and begin typing, any value already in the cell is overwritten.

2. Select E3..E14. Quattro Pro inserts the block address after the opening parenthesis.

3. Type a closing parenthesis, and click the ✓ button. Quattro Pro displays the result 822216.79. If you format this entry as currency with two decimal places and widen the column, the entry looks the same as the one in cell E15—$822,216.79.

Using References to Formula Cells in Other Formulas

After you create a formula in one cell, you can use its result in other formulas simply by referencing its cell. To see how this works, follow these steps:

1. Select B1, and type a plus sign.

Capital letters

When you type an @function name, such as @SUM, in the input line, you don't have to type it in capital letters. Quattro Pro capitalizes the @function name for you when you finish entering the @function. If Quattro Pro does not respond in this way, you have probably entered the @function name or its syntax incorrectly.

2. Click cell A1, which contains the @SUM function you just entered, type a / (the division operator), and then type *11*.

3. Click the ✓ button. Quattro Pro divides the result of the @SUM function by 11 and displays the result—the average of the invoice amounts—in cell B1.

Naming Cells and Blocks

Many of the calculations that you might want to perform in this notebook—for example, calculating each invoice amount as a percentage of total sales—will use the total you have just entered in cell A1. You can include a copy of the @SUM function now in cell A1 in these other calculations, or you can reference cell A1 to use the total. The latter method seems quick and simple, but what if you subsequently move the formula in cell A1 to another location. Quattro Pro gives you a way to reference this formula, no matter where you move it. You can assign cell A1 a name and then use the name in any calculations that involve the total.

You assign a name to a cell or block with the Names command on the Block menu. Follow these steps:

1. Select A1, choose Names from the Block menu, and then choose Create from the Names submenu. Quattro Pro displays the Create Name dialog box shown on the next page.

Assigning names to cells

> **POINT mode**
>
> In certain circumstances, you can save time by using Quattro Pro's POINT mode to enter cell and block references instead of typing them. For example, to enter a block address in a formula, you can simply select the block. The status line displays the POINT indicator while you make your selection. In many dialog boxes, you can activate an edit field and select a block to enter its address. When you start selecting the block, the dialog box shrinks to a title bar and moves out of the way above the input line. When you release the mouse button, the dialog box reappears, with the block address in the edit field.

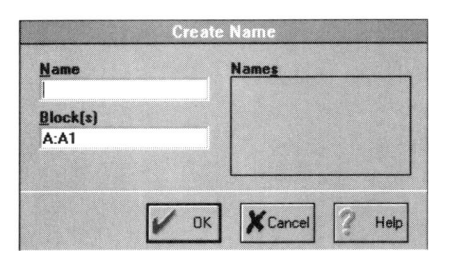

The reference for cell A1 is displayed in the Block(s) edit field.

2. Type the name *total* in the Name box, and click OK. Quattro Pro now refers to the cell by the name you just entered, as well as A1. You can use either designation in formulas.

To see how Quattro Pro uses names, try this:

Using names

1. Select E15, which currently contains the @SUM function inserted when you clicked the SpeedSum button earlier in the chapter.

2. Type +*total*, and then press Enter to record the entry in the cell. The notebook does not appear to have changed, but now instead of two @SUM functions, the notebook contains only one: You have told Quattro Pro to assign the value of the cell named TOTAL, which contains the @SUM function, to cell E15.

You can also assign names to cell blocks. Let's assign the name AMOUNT_OF_SALE to the cells containing amounts in column E.

Cell-naming conventions

Certain rules apply when you name cells or blocks. Names can have up to 15 characters and can contain any letter, number, or punctuation mark and some special characters. Don't use mathematical operators, the dollar sign, parentheses, just numbers (for example, 245), and number/letter combinations that can be construed as cell references (such as B1). Use underscore characters (_) to represent spaces. For example, instead of assigning TOTALS 1992 as a name, use TOTALS_1992 instead. Quattro Pro does not distinguish between uppercase and lowercase letters, so Totals and TOTALS are equivalent. Quattro Pro always displays names in uppercase letters.

1. Select E3..E14, and choose Names and then Create from the Block menu. Again, Quattro Pro displays the Create Name dialog box.

   Assigning names to blocks

2. Enter *amount_of_sale* in the Name edit field, and click OK to assign the name.

When you assign a name to a cell or block, Quattro Pro automatically replaces cell and block references in the notebook with the assigned name. Let's check:

Automatic reference updating

1. Select A1 to display its contents in the input line. Quattro Pro has replaced the block reference in the @SUM function with AMOUNT_OF_SALE.

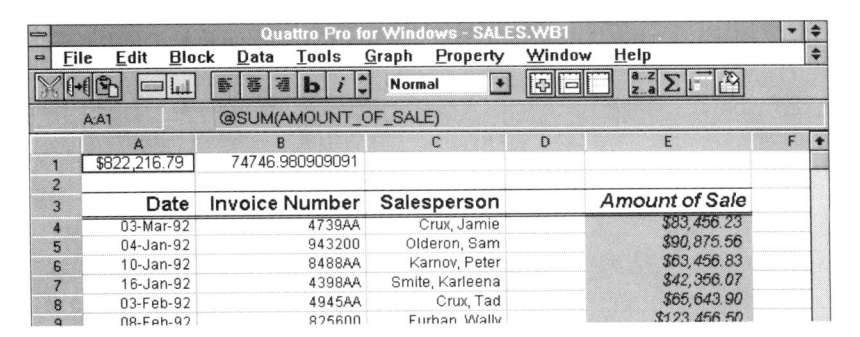

2. Select B1, and notice that Quattro Pro has also replaced the reference in the averaging formula with the name TOTAL.

Efficient Data Display

Before we discuss other calculations you might want to perform in this notebook, let's look at ways to format information to make it easier to read at a glance. We'll show you how to make the results of your calculations stand out from your data and how to format the data itself so that it is neat and consistent. As your notebooks grow in complexity, you'll find that paying attention to such details will keep you oriented and help others understand your results.

Linking with names

You can use names to refer to cells and blocks in other notebooks, even ones that are not currently open. See page 85 for more information about linking notebooks in this way.

Creating a Calculation Area

Usually when you create a notebook, you are interested not so much in the individual pieces of information as in the results of the calculations you perform on the pieces. The notebook page you are working with now fits neatly on one screen, but often one page can include several screenfuls of information. It's a good idea to design your notebooks so that the important information is easily accessible, and it helps if this information is always in a predictable location. For these reasons, we leave room in the top-left corner of our notebook pages for a calculation area. This habit is useful because:

- We don't have to scroll around looking for totals and other results because we always know where to find them.
- We can print just the calculation area to get a report of the most pertinent information.
- We can easily jump to the calculation area from anywhere in the notebook by pressing Home to move to cell A1.

Let's create an area at the top of page A of the SALES.WB1 notebook for a title and a set of calculations. We'll start by freeing up some space at the top of the notebook page:

1. Select A1..E14, and use the Cut and Paste commands or Drag and Drop editing to move the selection to A10..E23. Click Yes when Quattro Pro asks whether you want to overwrite non-blank cells. (The nonblank cell you are overwriting is the formula in cell E15.) Your screen now looks like this:

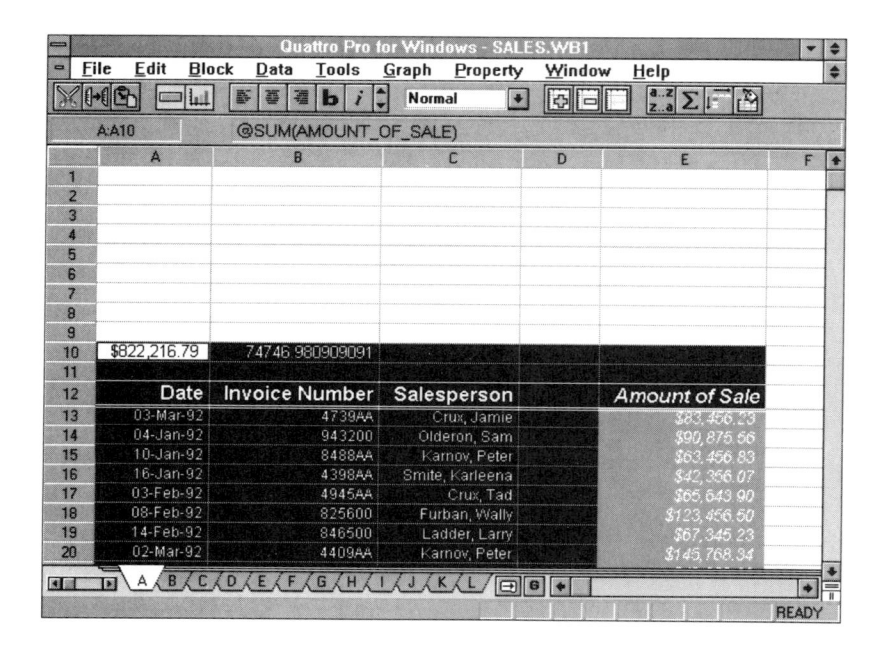

Chapter 2 Analyzing Income

As you can see, Quattro Pro can handle overlapping cut and paste areas without garbling the results. Now let's enter the notebook title:

2. Select B1, type *Preliminary Sales Analysis*, and press Down Arrow.

3. With cell B2 selected, type *'1st Quarter 1992*, and press Down Arrow.

Now that we have created a calculation area, let's move the calculation in cell A10. Follow these steps:

1. Select A4, type *Total Sales*, and then press Enter.

2. Select A10, click the Cut button on the SpeedBar, select cell B4, and click the Paste button.

3. Select B10, and press Del (or Delete) to erase the entry.

More Formatting Techniques

In Chapter 1, you learned how to format all the entries in a block at once by using the SpeedFormat button on the SpeedBar. In this section, we'll show you how to make minor changes one step at a time.

First, we'll set off the calculation area. With Quattro Pro, you can get really fancy, using different fonts, borders, and shading to draw attention to calculation results. We'll start by adding a set of double lines above the area:

1. Select A3..E3, and right-click the block.

Adding borders

2. In the Object Inspector, select the Line Drawing property to display this dialog box:

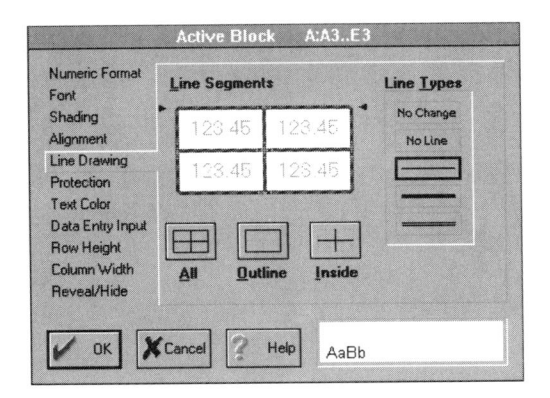

3. Select the double line in the Line Types box, click the top of the Line Segments diagram, and click OK. Quattro Pro puts a double line at the top of the block.

Now let's do something with the labels:

Changing fonts and sizes

1. Right-click cell B1, and select the Font property from the block Object Inspector. Quattro Pro displays this dialog box:

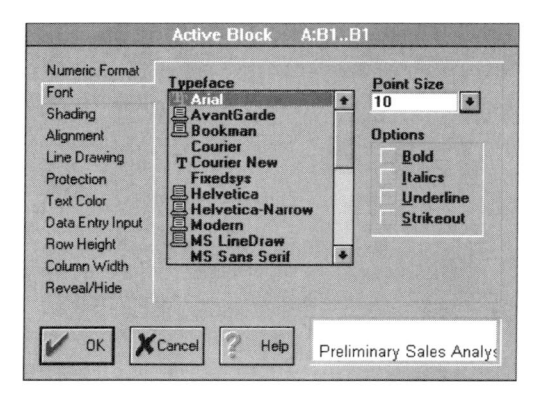

2. Select 18 from the drop-down Point Size list and Bold from the Options list. Click OK. Notice that the height of row 1 increases to accommodate the larger font.

3. Right-click cell B2, and select the Font property again. This time, select 14 from the Point Size drop-down list and Bold and Italics from the Options list. Click OK.

Boldface

4. Select A4..A8, and click the Bold button on the SpeedBar. Why did we tell you to select the empty cells below the Total Sales label before applying the bold format? Try this:

5. Select A5, type *Average Sale*, and press Enter. The new label is bold because we have already applied the bold format to cell A5.

6. Use any of the techniques you learned in Chapter 1 to widen column A so that you can see both of the labels you have entered (refer to page 28). Here's how your notebook page looks now:

Chapter 2 Analyzing Income

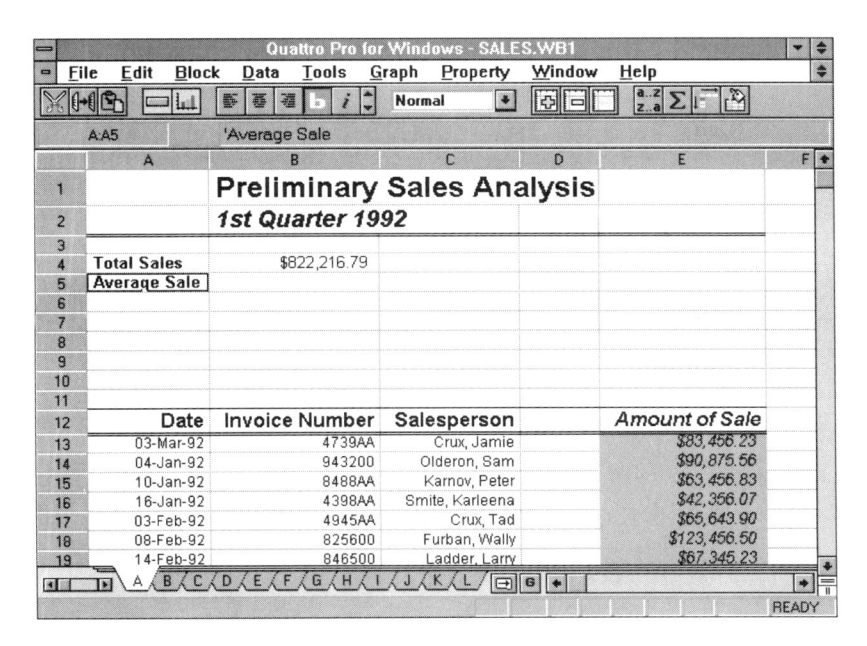

[Screenshot: Quattro Pro for Windows - SALES.WB1 showing Preliminary Sales Analysis, 1st Quarter 1992, with Total Sales $822,216.79 and a list of sales data]

From now on, adjust the column widths as necessary to see your work, and be sure to save your work regularly.

Using Styles

In Quattro Pro, you can group cell formats together as styles. Quattro Pro has 11 built-in styles that can quickly change the way cells look. The names of these 11 styles are displayed in the Style drop-down list box on the SpeedBar, as shown here:

Built-in styles

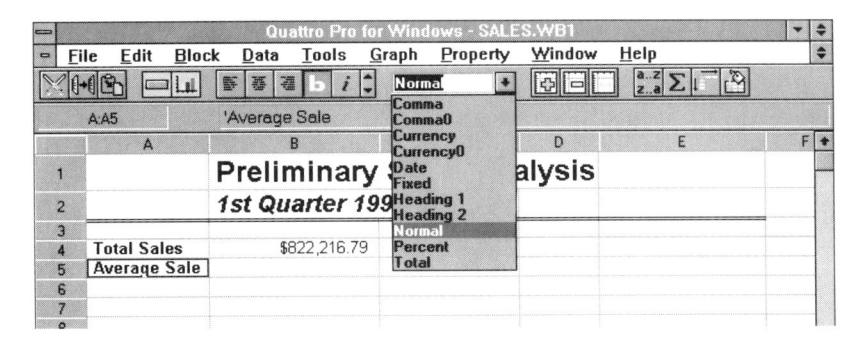

[Screenshot: Quattro Pro for Windows showing the Style drop-down list with options: Comma, Comma0, Currency, Currency0, Date, Fixed, Heading 1, Heading 2, Normal, Percent, Total]

The 11 styles change settings in the selected block's Object Inspector and produce the following effects:

- The Normal style sets Numeric Format and Alignment to General, Font to 10-point Arial, Shading to White, Line Drawing to None, and Text Color to Black. It also turns on Protection. By default, all cells in a notebook are originally formatted with the Normal style.

Font options

The fonts listed in the Font property of the block Object Inspector depend on the resolution of your screen, your Windows version, which fonts were installed with Windows, and which additional printer fonts are installed. Use the display in the bottom-right corner of the Object Inspector to experiment with combinations of font, size, and formatting options before you apply a format to the selected cells.

- The Comma style inserts commas in values greater than 999 to group digits into threes.
- The Comma0 style formats numeric values the same way as the Comma style but truncates the display of numbers to the right of the decimal point. Underlying values are unchanged.
- The Currency style adds a dollar sign in front of values, uses commas to group digits by threes, and displays two decimal places (cents).
- The Currency0 style formats numeric values the same way as the Currency style but truncates the display of numbers to the right of the decimal point. Underlying values are unchanged.
- The Date style sets the date format to the one selected in the Formats Defined section of the block Object Inspector.
- The Fixed style sets numeric values in the selected block to a fixed number of decimal places, as defined by the setting in the block Object Inspector.
- The Heading 1 style sets the Font property to 18-point Arial Bold.
- The Heading 2 style sets Font to 12-point Arial Bold.
- The Percent style displays the value as a percentage and appends a percent sign.
- The Total style inserts a double line above the active block.

Negative dollar values

To display negative dollar values with a minus sign instead of parentheses, right-click the Quattro Pro title bar to open the application Object Inspector. Select the International property, select Signed in the Negative Values section, and then click OK.

Sharing styles

You can share a style you create in one notebook with another notebook. Simply copy a cell formatted with the style, and paste it in the destination notebook. The style travels with the copied cell.

Chapter 2 Analyzing Income

As you can see, most of the built-in styles change just one element of a cell's formatting. You can redefine any built-in style to suit your needs. You can also create your own styles.

Applying a style from the Style drop-down list is a simple matter of selecting the cell or block you want to format and then selecting the desired style from the list box. Try this:

1. Select A9..E9, and select Total from the Style list. The block now looks like A3..E3.

   Applying styles

2. Select B4..B8, and select Currency from the Style list. Now any entries you make in this block will automatically be displayed as dollars and cents.

Using styles can save you a lot of formatting time. For example, if you always format currency to be displayed in bold italics with two decimal places, you can create a style (or redefine one of Quattro Pro's built-in styles) that applies these formats. Here's how:

1. Select B4..B8 if it is not already selected, and choose Define Style from the Edit menu to display this dialog box:

   Creating styles

2. In the Define Style For edit field, enter a name for the style—in this case, type *My Currency*. Each button in the Included Properties box displays the options you see if you select the corresponding property in the block Object Inspector. For example, clicking the Alignment button in the Included Properties box displays the same options as selecting the Alignment property in the block Object Inspector.

3. Click the check box in front of the Font button to activate it, and then click the Font button.

4. In the Font dialog box, select the Bold and Italics options, and click OK.

5. Click OK again to close the Define/Modify Style dialog box and return to the notebook.

6. Click the arrow to the right of the Style box on the SpeedBar. Quattro Pro has added My Currency to the Style list, so select the new style to apply it to B4..B8. Here's the result:

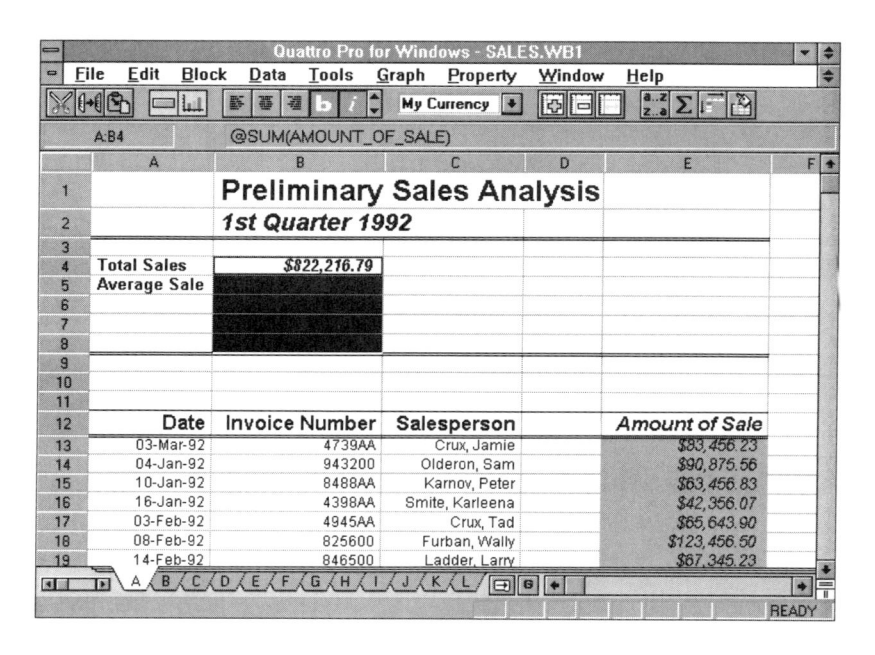

More Calculations

Now we'll move back to the calculation area and perform some more calculations on the sales data, starting with the average sale.

Averaging Values

To find the average amount for the invoices we've entered in this notebook, we'll use Quattro Pro's @AVG function. We'll also show you how to use the @Function list to select from a list of @functions available in Quattro Pro.

1. Select B5, and activate the input line by clicking it or pressing F2. Notice that Quattro Pro replaces the fourth and fifth buttons on the SpeedBar with two different buttons.

Underlying vs. displayed

After you apply a format, the value in the cell might look different from the value in the input line. For example, 345.6789 is displayed in its cell as $345.68 when you apply the Currency format. When performing calculations, Quattro Pro uses the value that appears in the input line, called the underlying value, not the displayed value.

Chapter 2 Analyzing Income

2. Click the @ button. Quattro Pro displays this dialog box:

Displaying a list of functions

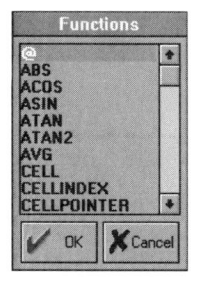

3. Select AVG, and click OK. The input line now looks like this:

The @AVG function

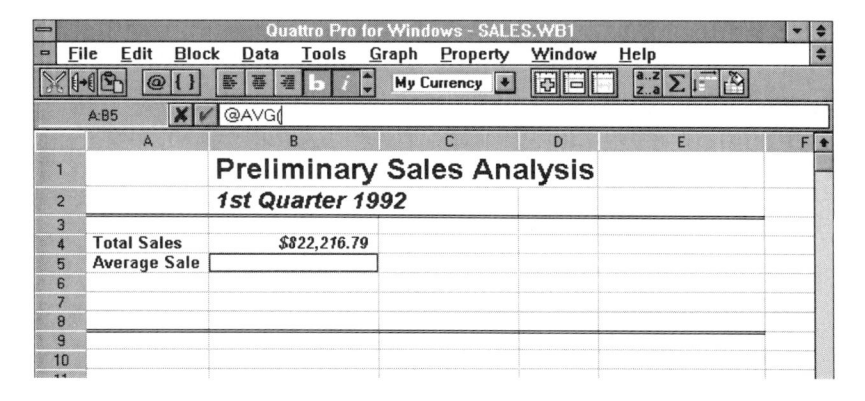

Quattro Pro has entered the @AVG function in the input line with an opening parenthesis, waiting for input from you.

4. Select E13..E23, and type a close parenthesis. The input line now looks as shown on the next page.

Custom numeric formats

You can create your own numeric formats or modify an existing format to meet special formatting needs. A detailed discussion of creating custom numeric formats could take an entire chapter, but here are the basic steps: Enter a value in a cell, and right-click the cell to open its Object Inspector. Then select User Defined in the Numeric Format property. Select a format that resembles the one you want to create. (If none of the formats is similar to the one you want, press Del to clear the Formats Defined edit field, and start from scratch.) Use N to start a number format and T to start a time or date format. Use 0s as required digit placeholders and 9s as optional digit placeholders. Use periods, commas, the percent sign, the dollar sign, and other symbols as you normally would. Also enter any text that you want to be part of the format. For example, if the value is 124 and you want Quattro Pro to display *You owe me $124.00* in the cell, you would create this format:

N You owe me $9,999.00

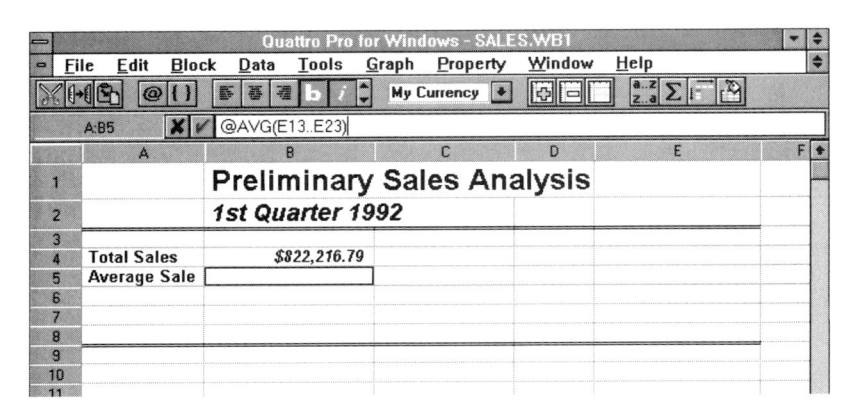

5. Click the ✓ button to record the formula in cell B5. Quattro Pro displays the result $74,746.98.

Identifying Highest and Lowest Sales

Quattro Pro provides two @functions that instantly identify the highest and lowest values in a group. To understand the benefits of these @functions, imagine that the SALES.WB1 notebook contains data from not 11 but 111 invoices! Let's start with the highest sale:

1. Select A6, type *Highest Sale*, and then press Right Arrow to enter the label and select cell B6.

The @MAX function

2. Activate the input line, and click the @ button. Scroll and select MAX, and click OK.

3. Select E13..E23, type a close parenthesis, and press Enter. Quattro Pro displays the highest sale, $145,768.34, in cell B6.

Now for the formula for the lowest sale, which we'll type in the input line:

1. Select A7, type *Lowest Sale*, and press Right Arrow.

The @MIN function

2. Type *@MIN(E13..E23)*, and press Enter. Quattro Pro displays the result, $11,256.90, in cell B7.

Calculating with Names

The last calculation we'll make with this set of data involves the Total Sales value from cell B4. As a gross indicator of sales expenses, let's calculate the total sales commission:

1. First, insert a couple of new rows in the calculation area by dragging through the borders for rows 8 and 9 and clicking the Insert button on the SpeedBar.

2. Select A8, type *Commission*, and press Right Arrow.

3. In cell B8, type *5%*, and click the ✓ button. Because the cell is formatted with the My Currency style, the entry appears as $0.05.

4. To correct the display of the entry, select Percent from the Style list.

5. With cell B8 still selected, choose Names and then Create from the Block menu. Type *Commission*, and click OK.

6. Select A9, type *Sales Expense*, and press Right Arrow.

7. In cell B9, type *+total*commission*, and press Enter. Quattro Pro multiplies the value in the cell named TOTAL (B4) by the value in the cell named COMMISSION (B8) and displays the result, $41,110.84, in cell B9.

8. Now select B8, type *6%*, and press Enter. The value in cell B9 changes to reflect the new commission rate, as shown here:

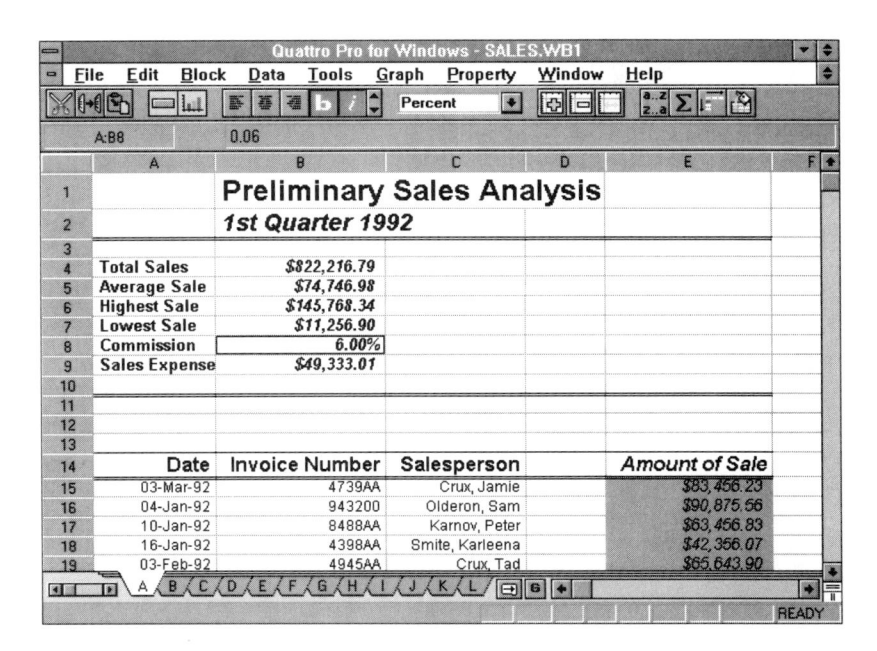

If a hundred calculations throughout the notebook involved the name COMMISSION, Quattro Pro would have adjusted all their results to reflect this one change.

Formulas That Make Decisions

There will be times when you want Quattro Pro to carry out one task under certain circumstances and another task if those circumstances don't apply. To give Quattro Pro this kind of instruction, you use the @IF function.

Using the @IF Function

The @IF function

In its simplest form, the @IF function tests the condition of a cell and does one thing if the condition is positive (true) and another if the condition is negative (false). It requires three arguments: the condition, the action to perform if the condition is true, and the action to perform if the condition is false. You supply the arguments one after the other within the @function's parentheses, separating them with commas (no spaces). Try this:

1. Select D4, and type *@IF*. Notice that Quattro Pro displays @IF (condition, true, false) at the left end of the status line to remind you that the @IF function requires three arguments.

2. Complete the formula by typing the following, and then click the ✓ button:

   (B4=0,"TRUE","FALSE")

   Quattro Pro checks whether the value of cell B4 is 0 (the condition), and because it isn't, it bypasses TRUE (the action to perform if the condition is true) and displays FALSE (the action to perform if the condition is false) in cell D4.

3. With cell D4 still selected, press F2 to activate the input line, highlight *=0*, type *<1000000*, and click the ✓ button. The entry in cell D4 instantly changes from FALSE to TRUE, because the value in cell B4 is less than 1 million (in other words, the condition is now true).

In this example, the test Quattro Pro performed was a simple evaluation of the value in a cell. However, you can also build conditions that involve other @functions. Recall that the last

Operators

Here is a list of operators you can use with the @IF function:

= < > <> >= <=

You can also use #AND#, #OR#, and #NOT#. For example, the following formula @IF(B4=0#AND#B5=5,"Yes","No") displays Yes only if both conditions are true. This formula @IF(B4=0#OR#B=5,"Yes","No") displays Yes if either condition is true.

Chapter 2 Analyzing Income

two characters of the invoice numbers in column B of the notebook indicate whether the sale originated in your company's East or West office. Suppose you want to assign East and West entries to each invoice so that you can compare the performance of the two offices. Follow these steps to experiment with a more complex @IF example:

1. Select D14, type *Office*, and press Down Arrow. Quattro Pro displays the label in large bold type because the formats from the old column D were applied to the new column D when you inserted it in Chapter 1.

2. In cell D15, type the following, and click the ✓ button:

   @IF(@RIGHT(B15,2)="AA","East","West")

   You have told Quattro Pro to look at the two characters at the right end of the value in cell B15 and, if they are AA, to enter the label East in cell D15. If they are not AA, Quattro Pro is to enter West. Here's the result:

The @RIGHT function

	A	B	C	D	E
12					
13					
14	Date	Invoice Number	Salesperson	Office	Amount of Sale
15	03-Mar-92	4739AA	Crux, Jamie	East	$83,456.23
16	04-Jan-92	943200	Olderon, Sam		$90,875.56
17	10-Jan-92	8488AA	Karnov, Peter		$63,456.83
18	16-Jan-92	4398AA	Smite, Karleena		$42,356.07
19	03-Feb-92	4945AA	Crux, Tad		$65,643.90
20	08-Feb-92	825600	Furban, Wally		$123,456.50
21	14-Feb-92	846500	Ladder, Larry		$67,345.23
22	02-Mar-92	4409AA	Karnov, Peter		$145,768.34
23	12-Mar-92	8867AA	Crux, Jamie		$43,256.23
24	23-Mar-92	875600	Ladder, Larry		$11,256.90
25	30-Mar-92	479300	Furban, Wally		$85,345.00

Using Nested @IF Functions

When constructing tests, you can use @IF functions within @IF functions. Called nested @functions, these formulas add another dimension to the complexity of the decisions Quattro Pro can make. Turn the page for a quick demonstration.

Text values as arguments

When entering text values as arguments in an @function or a formula, you must enclose them in quotation marks. Otherwise, Quattro Pro thinks the text is a block name. For example,

@RIGHT("Quat",2)

gives the value "at," but

@RIGHT(Quat,2)

results in an error—unless the block name QUAT happens to be defined in the notebook.

Creating nested functions

1. Insert a new column between columns A and B by clicking column B's border and then clicking the Insert button.

2. Enter the column label *Quarter* in cell B14.

3. Select B15..B25, and select Normal from the Style list.

4. Select B15, and type the following formula on one line:

The @MONTH function

@IF(@MONTH(A15)<4,1,@IF(@MONTH(A15)<7,2, @IF(@MONTH(A15)<10,3,4)))

5. Check your typing, paying special attention to all the parentheses, and then click the ✓ button.

You have told Quattro Pro to check the month component of the date in cell A15. If it is less than 4, Quattro Pro is to display 1 in the corresponding cell in the Quarter column. If the month is not less than 4 (in other words, the first condition is false) but it is less than 7, Quattro Pro is to display 2 in the Quarter column. If it is not less than 7 (the second condition is false) but it is less than 10, Quattro Pro is to display 3. Otherwise (if the third condition is false), Quattro Pro is to display 4. If you have typed the formula correctly, Quattro Pro enters 1 in cell B15.

Copying Formulas

The @IF functions you have just entered are pretty arduous to type, even for good typists. Fortunately, you don't have to enter them more than once. Using Copy and Paste, you can duplicate the formulas in other cells, and the references will change automatically to keep the formulas correct.

1. Select B15, and click the Copy button.

Copying down a block

2. Select B16..B25, and click the Paste button. Quattro Pro copies the @IF formula into the selected block. Notice in the input line that all the references to cell A15 have changed to cell A16.

3. Use the same technique to copy the formula in cell E15 to the block E16..E25. The notebook now looks like this:

Chapter 2 Analyzing Income

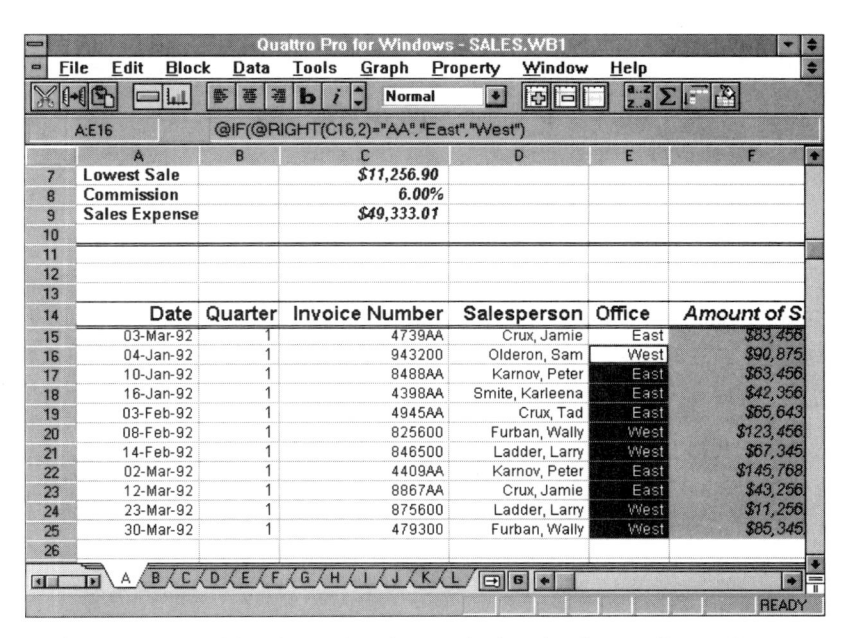

	A	B	C	D	E	F
7	Lowest Sale		$11,256.90			
8	Commission		6.00%			
9	Sales Expense		$49,333.01			
10						
11						
12						
13						
14	Date	Quarter	Invoice Number	Salesperson	Office	Amount of S
15	03-Mar-92	1	4739AA	Crux, Jamie	East	$83,456
16	04-Jan-92	1	943200	Olderon, Sam	West	$90,875
17	10-Jan-92	1	8488AA	Karnov, Peter	East	$63,456
18	16-Jan-92	1	4398AA	Smite, Karleena	East	$42,356
19	03-Feb-92	1	4945AA	Crux, Tad	East	$65,643
20	08-Feb-92	1	825600	Furban, Wally	West	$123,456
21	14-Feb-92	1	846500	Ladder, Larry	West	$67,345
22	02-Mar-92	1	4409AA	Karnov, Peter	East	$145,768
23	12-Mar-92	1	8867AA	Crux, Jamie	East	$43,256
24	23-Mar-92	1	875600	Ladder, Larry	West	$11,256
25	30-Mar-92	1	479300	Furban, Wally	West	$85,345

4. Select E15, and look at the formula in the input line. Quattro Pro has changed the original formula

   @IF(@RIGHT(B15,2)="AA","East","West")

   to

   @IF(@RIGHT(C15,2)="AA","East","West")

   Quattro Pro changed the reference to account for the addition of the Quarter column. If you click cell E16, you'll see that when you copied and pasted the formula from E15, Quattro Pro changed the reference so that it refers to cell C16, not C15.

   By default, Quattro Pro uses relative references in its formulas. Relative references refer to cells by their position in relation to the cell containing the formula. So when you copied the formula in cell E15 to cell E16, Quattro Pro changed the reference in the formula from C15 to C16—the cell in the same row and two columns to the left of the cell containing the formula. If you were to copy the formula in cell E15 to F15, Quattro Pro would change the reference from C15 to D15 so that the formula would continue to reference the cell in the same relative position.

   Relative references

   When you don't want a reference to be copied as a relative reference, as it was in the preceding examples, you need to

Absolute references

use an absolute reference. Absolute references refer to cells by their fixed position in the notebook. To make a reference absolute, you add dollar signs before its column letter and row number. For example, to change the reference C4..C9 to an absolute reference, you would enter it as C4..C9. You could then move a formula that contained this reference anywhere on the notebook, and it would always refer to the block C4..C9.

References can also be partially relative and partially absolute. For example, $C3 has an absolute column reference and a relative row reference, and C$3 has a relative column reference and an absolute row reference.

Printing Notebooks

If your primary purpose in learning Quattro Pro is to be able to manipulate your own information and come up with results that will guide your decision-making, your notebooks might never need to leave your computer. If, on the other hand, you want to sway the decisions of your colleagues or you need to prepare reports for your board of directors, you will probably need printed copies of your notebooks. Now is a good time to cover how to preview and print a Quattro Pro notebook.

Print Preview

Usually, you'll want to preview your notebooks before you print them to make sure that they fit neatly on the page or break across pages in logical places. This is where Print Preview comes in handy. In Print Preview, you can change margins, column widths, and the basic page layout, but you cannot make any modifications to the values in the notebook. Let's preview SALES.WB1:

Zoom view

Instead of using Print Preview, you can use Zoom view to zoom in and out of areas of a notebook. Right-click the notebook's title bar to open the notebook Object Inspector. Select the Zoom Factor property, and then select a Zoom Percentage (25% through 200%). The larger magnifications might be useful for users with impaired vision, and the smaller ones give you an overview of your notebook's structure.

1. Make certain only one cell is selected, and choose Print Preview from the File menu. (If you select a block before you choose the command, Quattro Pro assumes you want to preview and print only that block.) The Print Preview window opens, with a miniature version of the printed notebook displayed, as shown here:

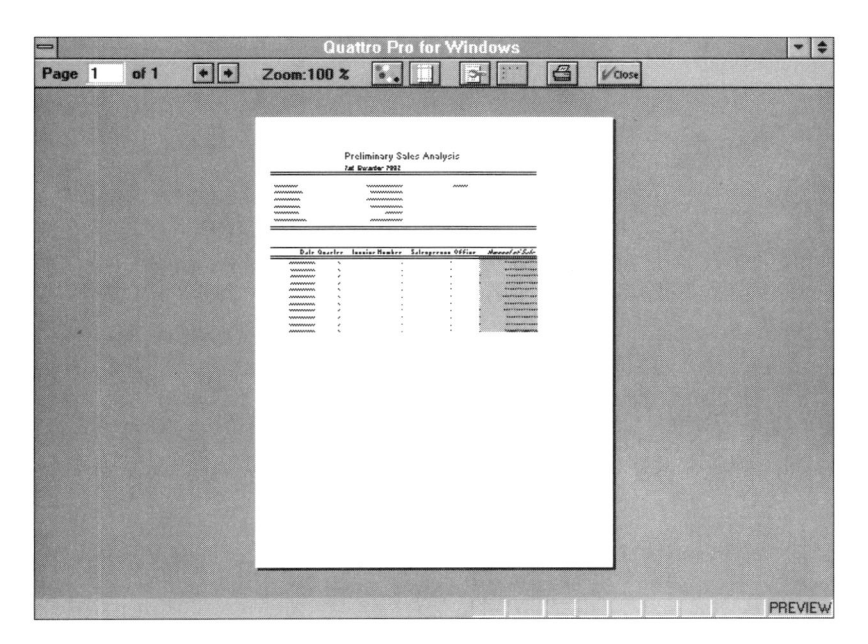

Notice that Quattro Pro will print only the rectangular block needed to hold all the cells containing entries.

2. Move the mouse pointer over the page. The pointer changes to a small magnifying glass.

3. To examine part of the page in more detail, move the magnifying glass over that part, and click the left mouse button. Quattro Pro zooms in on that portion of the page. You can click again to zoom in further (up to 1600%). Right-click to zoom out.

Zooming in and out

Printer setup

If your computer can access more than one printer, or if you need to set up your printer to print with Quattro Pro, choose Printer Setup from the File menu, and select the printer you want to use or adjust. Then click the Setup button, and make the necessary settings in each printer's Setup dialog box before trying to print. Any changes you make in these dialog boxes remain in effect for printing in all Windows applications.

Setting Up the Pages

For presentation purposes, you might want to make changes to the way Quattro Pro prints out your notebook. For example, you might want to include a header at the top of the page and/or a footer at the bottom. You make these changes in the Spreadsheet Page Setup dialog box, which Quattro Pro displays when you choose Page Setup from the File menu. When you are in Print Preview, you can also access this dialog box directly.

1. Click the Setup button at the top of the Print Preview window to display the Spreadsheet Page Setup dialog box:

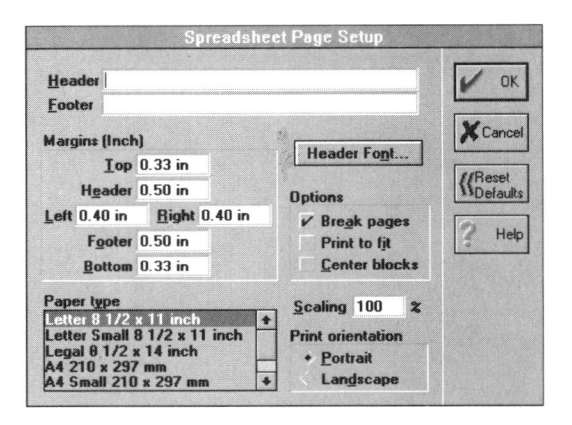

Header and footer codes

When these header and footer codes are inserted into the Header and Footer fields in the Spreadsheet Page Setup dialog box, they do the following:

#ds	Prints short date
#Ds	Prints long date
#p	Prints current page number
#P	Prints total pages in printout
&f	Prints name of notebook
|	Centers the text that follows it
||	Right-aligns the text that follows it

Setting page breaks

Quattro Pro automatically figures where it should break pages for printing. If you want to print the calculation area on one page and the supporting data on another, or if you need to control where the pages break in a multi-page notebook, select the cell below the row at which you want Quattro Pro to break the page, and choose Insert Break from the Block menu. A new row appears containing a page break symbol. (Manual page breaks don't appear in Print Preview.) To remove a manual page break, simply delete the row.

2. To add a header, you enter text and codes in the appropriate edit fields at the top of the dialog box. In the Header field, type |*Sales Analysis*. The vertical bar (|) tells Quattro Pro to center the text. By default, header and footer text is left-aligned.

   Adding headers

3. In the Footer field, type |*#p*. This code tells Quattro Pro to print the current page number, centered at the bottom of the page.

   Adding footers

4. Click the Header Font button. In the Select Font dialog box, select the Bold option, and click OK. This option makes both the header and footer text bold.

5. Select the Center Blocks option to horizontally center the header and footer on the printed page. Click OK to return to the Print Preview window, which now looks like this:

   Centering headers and footers

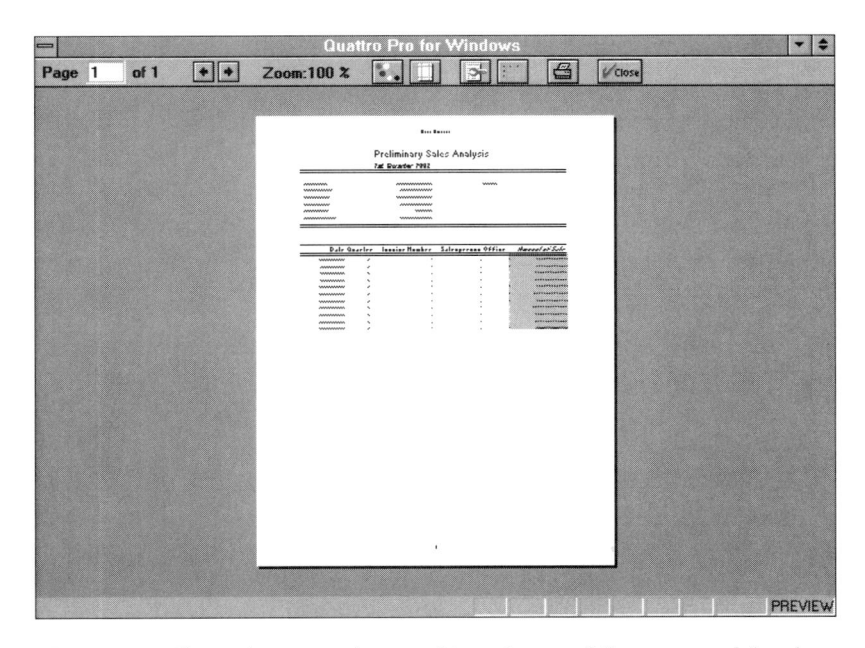

You can adjust the margins and header and footer positioning in the Print Preview window by clicking the Margin button to display guidelines and then manually moving the guidelines to increase or decrease the margins and the header and footer borders.

Setting margins

Exiting Print Preview

Printing from Print Preview

If you need to return to the notebook to make additional changes before printing, you can close the Print Preview window by clicking the Close button.

Getting Ready to Print

You can print directly from the Print Preview window by simply clicking the Print button. However, if you want to set any print options, you must print via the Spreadsheet Print dialog box, like this:

1. Click the Close button in Print Preview to return to the notebook window.

2. Choose Print from the File menu. Quattro Pro displays this Spreadsheet Print dialog box.

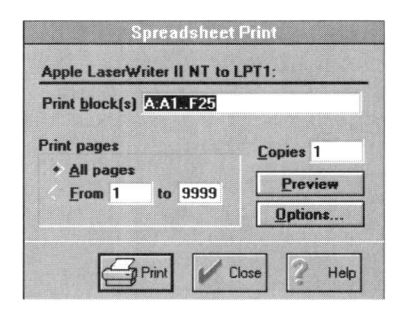

Repeating labels

To repeat row or column headings on all printed pages of a multi-page notebook, click the Options button in the Print Preview window, or choose the Print command from the File menu, and click the Options button. In the Spreadsheet Print Options dialog box, enter the reference for any cell in the row you want to use as a top heading and/or any cell in the column you want to use as a left heading in the appropriate edit fields. Then choose the block to be printed *without* the headings. If you select the headings as part of the print block, they will print twice.

3. In the Copies edit field, enter the number of copies to print. ← **Number of copies**

4. To print the entire notebook, leave the Print Block(s) setting as it is. Otherwise, indicate the blocks you want to print. ← **Specifying print blocks**

5. If you want to print all the notebook pages, leave the Print Pages option set to All Pages. Otherwise, indicate the pages in the From and To edit fields.

6. Check that your printer is ready to go, and then click the Print button. You can also click the Preview button to return to the Print Preview window or click Options to open the Spreadsheet Print Options dialog box.

That should do it. We've done a lot of work in this chapter, and you can now evaluate the results on paper. After looking at your printed notebook, be sure to save it again.

Other print options

When printing notebooks for your own purposes instead of presentation or display, gridlines and row and column borders can make the printed page easier to read. You can turn on these options in the Spreadsheet Print Options dialog box, accessed through Print Preview or the Spreadsheet Print dialog box. You can also choose to print formulas instead of formula results, by selecting the Cell Formulas option.

Several other options in the Spreadsheet Page Setup dialog box are worth noting. Print To Fit attempts to print a notebook on as few pages as possible by shrinking text. The Scaling setting lets you increase or decrease the size of notebook data on the printed page. Print Orientation lets you select between printing the notebook page vertically (Portrait, the default) or horizontally (Landscape).

Named print settings

If you find that you use several different print settings for one notebook, Quattro Pro has an answer to your woes. Just create each setting once, then choose Named Settings from the File menu. In the Named Print Settings dialog box, type a name for the print settings, and click Create. To change the settings assigned to a name, choose the command again, select the setting name, and click Update.

Extracting Information from a Database

Cloning Notebooks 64
Sorting Data 66
Adding Sort Codes 66
Using One Sort Key 67
Using Two Sort Keys 69
Using Three Sort Keys 70
Freezing Labels 71
Database Basics 72
Manipulating Records 74
Creating the Criteria Table 75
Entering Criteria 76
Locating and Deleting Records 77
Extracting Records 80
Using Group Mode 82
Using Database @Functions 84

Creating templates
Page 83

Defining groups
Page 83

Locating records
Page 77

Creating a series of dates
Page 65

Using the Fill command
Page 65

Turning on Group mode
Page 83

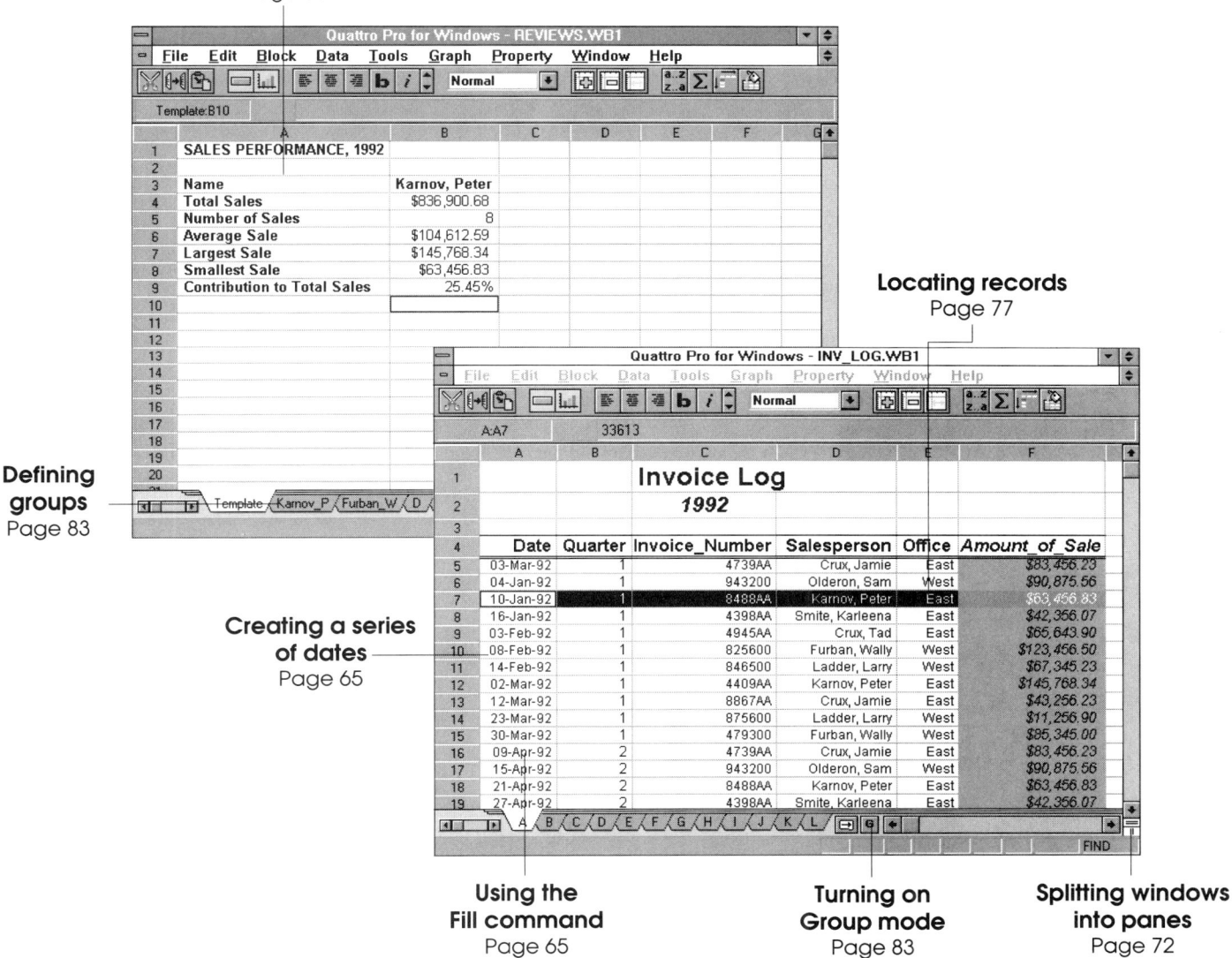

Splitting windows into panes
Page 72

To work efficiently with Quattro Pro, you need to know more than just how to input and format data. By planning ahead and putting to use some tried-and-true tricks and time-saving techniques, you can save yourself hours of tedious work at the computer. That's why we think it is important now to show you how to clone notebooks (use one notebook as the foundation for building another), sort and extract data, and link notebooks so that when you update one, all are updated. Where to begin? Let's start by creating an invoice log.

Cloning Notebooks

Using one notebook as the basis for another is an important time-saving technique. In this section, we will clone the SALES.WB1 notebook to create another notebook called INV_LOG.WB1. Then we'll use a few tricks to transform the new notebook into a simulated invoice log (a record of sales). If you need to create such a log for your work, you can key in real data. In Chapter 6, we show you how to automate the process of inputting this kind of information so that you are spared hours of typing. In the meantime, though, let's create a simulated log to give us a large notebook to manipulate in the other sections of this chapter. Follow these steps to create INV_LOG.WB1:

Duplicating notebooks

1. Locate and open SALES.WB1.

2. Delete the extraneous formula in cell E4, and choose Save As from the File menu.

3. In the File Name edit field, type *inv_log*, and click OK.

You now have two nearly identical notebooks saved under different names. A few alterations to INV_LOG.WB1 will give you a useable sample notebook.

1. Select C1, type *Invoice Log*, and press Down Arrow to both enter the text and select cell C2. Then type ^*1992*, and press Down Arrow. Notice that both entries retain the text formatting of the previous entries.

2. Select the borders for rows 3 through 12, and click the Delete button.

Chapter 3 Extracting Information from a Database 65

3. Select A5..F48, and click the Copy button. Then select A16, and click the Paste button.

4. Select A5..F26, and click the Copy button. Then select A27, and click the Paste button. You now have a log that contains 44 invoices.

Let's revise some of the invoice dates so that the log includes invoices for all the months of the year. Rather than changing dates manually, we'll take this opportunity to demonstrate the Fill command on the Block menu. Later in this chapter, we'll use this command to create a sequential set of numbers. Here, we'll use it to create a set of evenly spaced dates. (Obviously, if you were logging real invoices in this database, you would use the actual sale dates.) Follow these steps:

1. Select A16..A26, and choose the Fill command from the Block menu. Quattro Pro displays this dialog box:

Using the Fill command

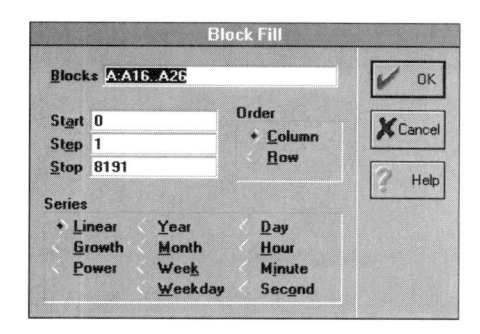

2. Delete the entry in the Start edit field, type *04/09/92*, select the entry, and press Ctrl-Shift-D to indicate that the entry is a date. Delete the entry in the Step edit field, and type *4*. Delete the entry in the Stop edit field, type *12/31/92*, select the entry, and press Ctrl-Shift-D. Then select the Weekday option in the Series box, and click OK. Quattro Pro uses the Start value as its starting point and creates a series of dates that are four business days apart (the Step value), skipping to Monday if a date falls on Saturday or Sunday.

Creating a series of dates

Calculating dates using weekdays

3. Select A27..A37, and again choose Fill from the Block menu. Notice that Quattro Pro has converted the dates you entered in the Start and Stop fields to date values.

4. Delete the value in the Start edit field, type *07/09/92*, select the entry, press Ctrl-Shift-D, and click OK.

5. Select A38..A48, choose Fill a third time, type *10/09/92* in the Start field, and click OK.

Notice that your notebook now contains invoices for all four quarters of the year. The formulas in column B have done their work and assigned the invoices to quarters based on the dates in column A.

This large notebook is ideal for demonstrating some of Quattro Pro's database features.

Sorting Data

The sales data in the notebook you created in Chapter 2 fits neatly on one screen. To find out which salesperson from the West office has made the highest single sale, you could simply look at the notebook. Getting that information from the notebook now on your screen is a little more difficult. Fortunately, Quattro Pro can quickly sort the entries in notebooks like this one, using up to five levels of sorting.

Adding Sort Codes

Before you sort any large notebook, you should ask yourself whether you might need to put the data back in its original order. If there is even a chance that you will, you should add sort codes to the notebook before you begin sorting. A sort

---

SpeedFill

You can use SpeedFill to quickly fill a block with values, labels, or formulas. If the first cell of the block contains a formula, SpeedFill simply copies it into all the cells of the block without altering any relative references. If the first cell contains a label that SpeedFill doesn't recognize as part of a series, it simply copies the label. If the label is part of a series, such as Monday or 1st, SpeedFill fills the block with succeeding members of the series. If the first cell contains a value, SpeedFill also treats it as the starting point in a series. If two or more of the cells at the beginning of the block contain entries, SpeedFill tries to find a pattern in the entries and repeats the pattern throughout the block. For example, entering *Monday* and *Wednesday* in the first two cells of a block causes SpeedFill to fill the block with the name of every other day.

code is a sequential number assigned to each row of entries. After sorting the entries, you can sort one more time on the basis of the sort code to put everything back where it was. Follow these steps to add sort codes to INV_LOG.WB1:

1. Insert a blank column in front of the Date column by clicking the column A border and then clicking the Insert button.

2. Select A4, type *Sort Code*, and press Down Arrow.

3. In cell A5, type *1*, and press Down Arrow.

4. In cell A6, type *2*, and press Enter.

5. Select A5..A48, and click the SpeedFill button. Quattro Pro uses the values in cells A5 and A6 as its starting point and inserts in the selected block a sequential set of numbers that continue the pattern established in A5 and A6, as shown here:

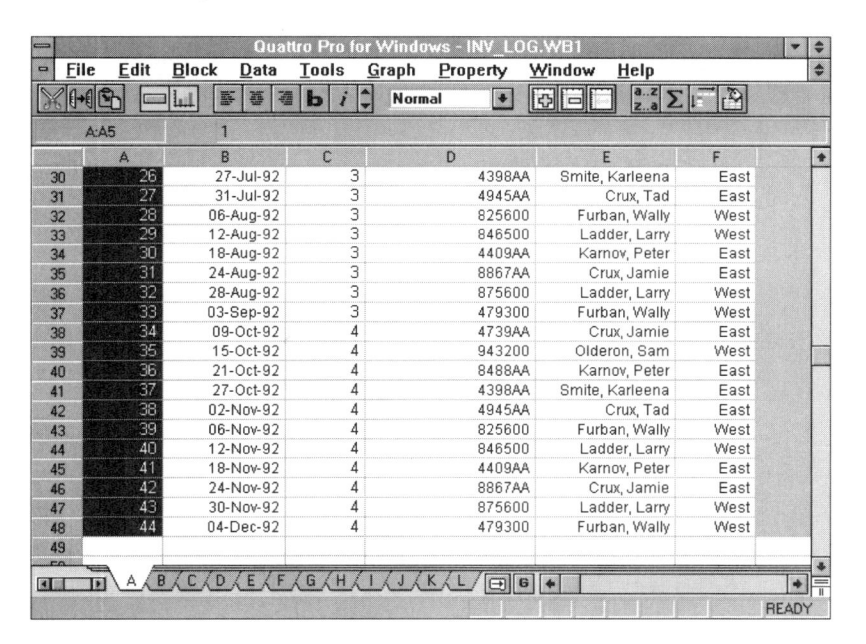

Creating a series of numbers

Now let's look at various ways you might want to sort the INV_LOG.WB1 notebook.

Using One Sort Key

The simplest sorting procedure is based on only one set of criteria, or sort key. You indicate which column or row Quattro Pro should use, and the program rearranges the selected block accordingly. Follow these steps to sort the data in INV_LOG.WB1 by regional office so that you can see how the process works:

1. Press Home to make sure only cell A1 is selected, and then choose Sort from the Data menu. Quattro Pro displays the Data Sort dialog box:

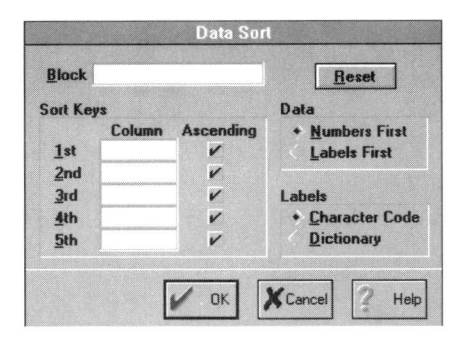

2. Enter A5..G48 in the Block edit field.

3. The Sort Keys box contains five edit fields in which you type sort key references. In the 1st edit field, designate the column you want Quattro Pro to use as the basis for the sort by entering the reference for any cell in column F of the table, such as F6. (You can also enter a reference by simply clicking a cell in the sort key column.)

4. Leave the sort order set to Ascending, and click OK. Here's the result:

Don't include labels

If you include the label row—in this case, row 4—in the block to be sorted, Quattro Pro sorts the labels along with the entries. As a result, the labels might end up in the middle of the notebook.

SpeedSort

To do a simple one-key ascending or descending sort, use the SpeedSort button on the SpeedBar. Select the block to sort, hold down Ctrl-Shift, and click anywhere in the sort key column. Then click the top half of the SpeedSort button to sort in ascending order, or click the bottom half to sort in descending order.

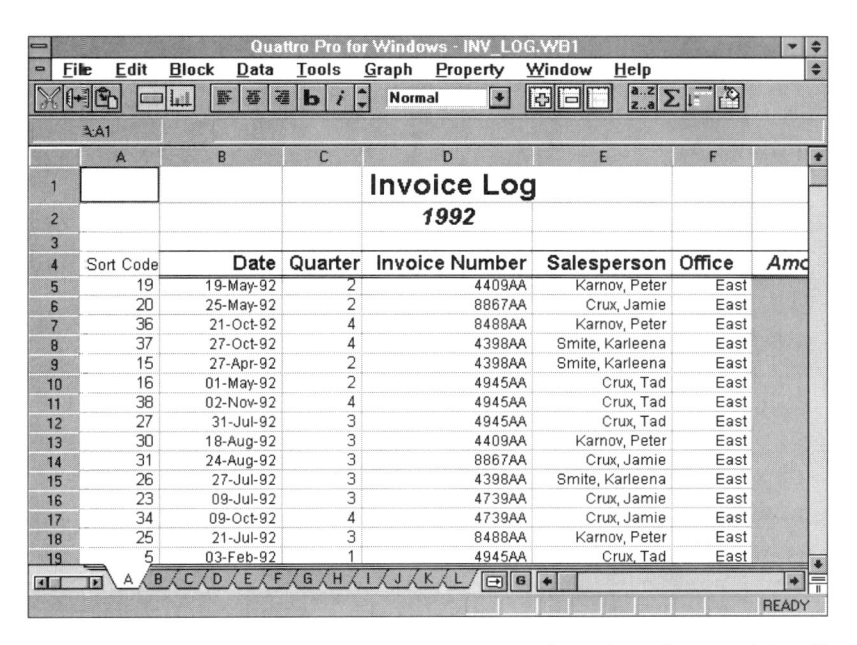

Chapter 3 Extracting Information from a Database   69

	A	B	C	D	E	F
1				Invoice Log		
2				1992		
3						
4	Sort Code	Date	Quarter	Invoice Number	Salesperson	Office
5	19	19-May-92	2	4409AA	Karnov, Peter	East
6	20	25-May-92	2	8867AA	Crux, Jamie	East
7	36	21-Oct-92	4	8488AA	Karnov, Peter	East
8	37	27-Oct-92	4	4398AA	Smite, Karleena	East
9	15	27-Apr-92	2	4398AA	Smite, Karleena	East
10	16	01-May-92	2	4945AA	Crux, Tad	East
11	38	02-Nov-92	4	4945AA	Crux, Tad	East
12	27	31-Jul-92	3	4945AA	Crux, Tad	East
13	30	18-Aug-92	3	4409AA	Karnov, Peter	East
14	31	24-Aug-92	3	8867AA	Crux, Jamie	East
15	26	27-Jul-92	3	4398AA	Smite, Karleena	East
16	23	09-Jul-92	3	4739AA	Crux, Jamie	East
17	34	09-Oct-92	4	4739AA	Crux, Jamie	East
18	25	21-Jul-92	3	8488AA	Karnov, Peter	East
19	5	03-Feb-92	1	4945AA	Crux, Tad	East

The invoice data is now sorted by regional office, with all the invoices for the East office coming before those for the West office.

Using Two Sort Keys

Now let's take things a step further and sort the invoices not only by regional office but also by salesperson.

1. Choose Sort from the Data menu again. The Data Sort dialog box has retained the entries you made for the previous sort operation.

Undoing a notebook sort

If a sort produces unexpected results and you decide to return your database to its previous order, simply choose Undo Sort Go from the Edit menu immediately after the sort.

Ascending vs. descending order

Ascending order places numbers before text, 1 before 2, and A before B. Descending order does just the opposite. It places text before numbers, B before A, and 2 before 1. To sort in descending order, deselect Ascending in the Data Sort dialog box.

Better "save" than sorry

Remember to save your notebook often, perhaps after each sort. You can use Save As to create a new notebook if you don't want to overwrite the results of one sort with the next.

2. Click the 2nd edit field, select a cell in column E, and click OK.

The table is now sorted by regional office and, within region, alphabetically by salesperson.

Using Three Sort Keys

Depending on the focus of your current analysis, you might want to sort INV_LOG.WB1 based on the Date or Quarter column. However, let's assume you are interested in each person's sales performance and add one more key to the sort. To sort by regional office, salesperson, and amount of sale, follow these steps:

1. Choose Sort from the Data menu.
2. Click the 3rd edit field, select a cell in column G, specify Descending sort order by clicking the Ascending box to deselect it, and click OK.

Now you can easily spot the highest sale for each salesperson in both regions. (We moved column A out of the way and adjusted the column widths so that you can see columns B through G.)

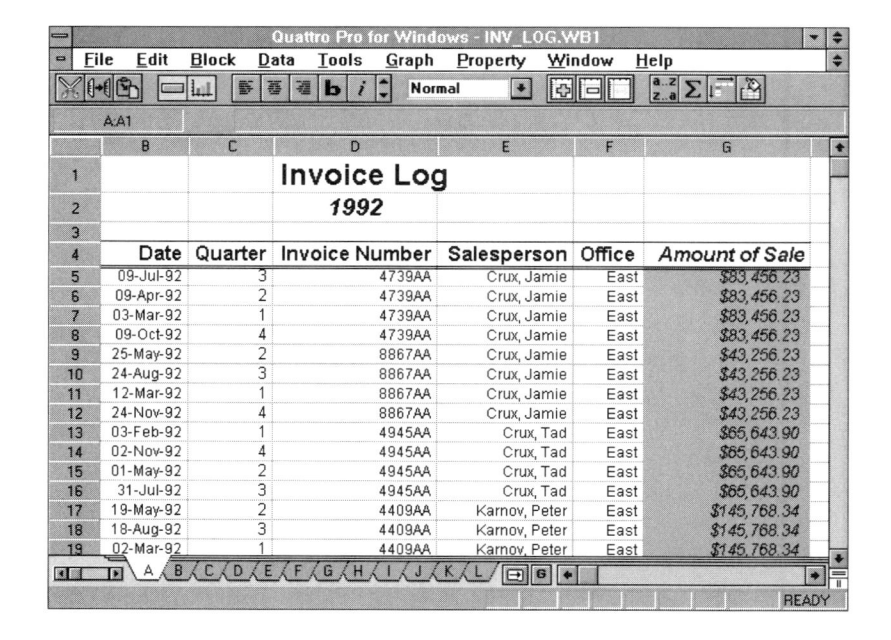

	Date	Quarter	Invoice Number	Salesperson	Office	Amount of Sale
5	09-Jul-92	3	4739AA	Crux, Jamie	East	$83,456.23
6	09-Apr-92	2	4739AA	Crux, Jamie	East	$83,456.23
7	03-Mar-92	1	4739AA	Crux, Jamie	East	$83,456.23
8	09-Oct-92	4	4739AA	Crux, Jamie	East	$83,456.23
9	25-May-92	2	8867AA	Crux, Jamie	East	$43,256.23
10	24-Aug-92	3	8867AA	Crux, Jamie	East	$43,256.23
11	12-Mar-92	1	8867AA	Crux, Jamie	East	$43,256.23
12	24-Nov-92	4	8867AA	Crux, Jamie	East	$43,256.23
13	03-Feb-92	1	4945AA	Crux, Tad	East	$65,643.90
14	02-Nov-92	4	4945AA	Crux, Tad	East	$65,643.90
15	01-May-92	2	4945AA	Crux, Tad	East	$65,643.90
16	31-Jul-92	3	4945AA	Crux, Tad	East	$65,643.90
17	19-May-92	2	4409AA	Karnov, Peter	East	$145,768.34
18	18-Aug-92	3	4409AA	Karnov, Peter	East	$145,768.34
19	02-Mar-92	1	4409AA	Karnov, Peter	East	$145,768.34

Freezing Labels

As you scroll through the invoice log to check how Quattro Pro has sorted the data, you'll probably find yourself wishing that the column labels didn't scroll out of sight. You can freeze the labels at the top of the screen like this:

1. Select B5, and choose Locked Titles from the Window menu to display this dialog box:

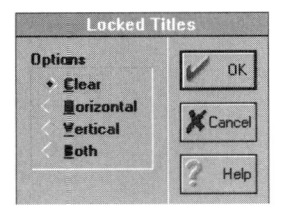

2. Select Horizontal, and click OK.

3. Back on the notebook, use the vertical scroll bar to scroll down through the data. The labels in row 4 remain in view while succeeding rows scroll up. In effect, the Locked Titles command allows you to view two different areas of your notebook, as you can see here:

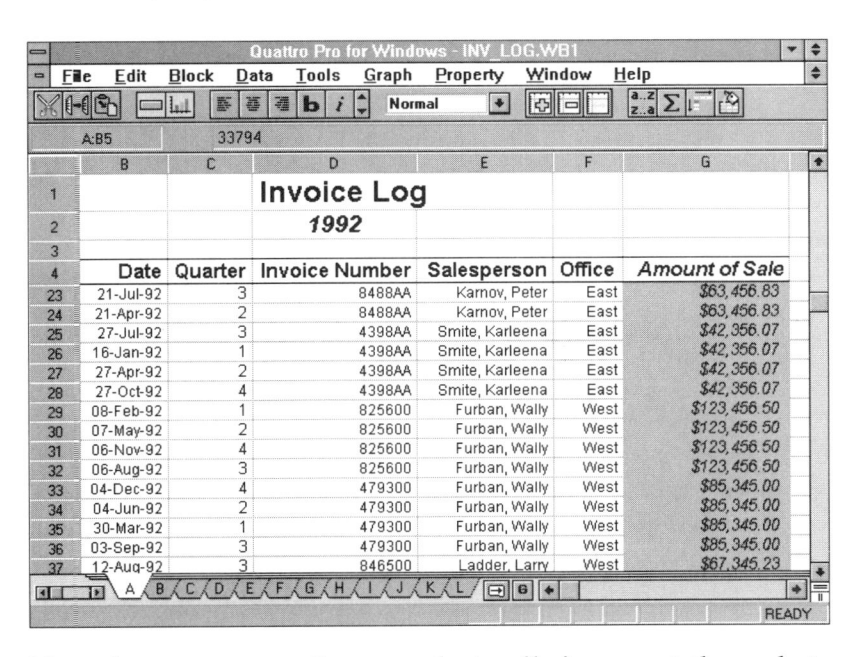

Note that you can no longer select cells in rows 1 through 4.

4. Scroll down to row 49, select G49, and click the SpeedSum button.

5. Use the Currency style in the Style list to format the total.

6. To turn off the locked titles, choose Locked Titles from the Window menu again, select Clear, and click OK.

Splitting windows into panes

Another way to achieve a similar effect is to split your notebook into panes. To create panes, you use the pane splitter at the junction of the vertical and horizontal scroll bars in the bottom-right corner of the notebook window. Click the horizontal lines in the pane splitter and drag up to create a horizontal split. Click the vertical lines and drag left to create a vertical split. You can then scroll the information in the panes independently.

Returning to a single pane

You might want to spend a few minutes experimenting with panes before you continue reading. To restore your notebook window to a single pane, drag the pane splitter back to its original position.

Database Basics

The invoice log is an organized collection of information about invoices. By common definition, it is a database.

A database is a table of related data with a rigid structure that enables you to easily locate and evaluate individual items of

---

A splitting alternative

Another way to split a window into panes is to select a split location on your notebook, choose Panes from the Window menu, select Horizontal or Vertical from the Window Panes dialog box, and then click OK. To restore your notebook window to a single pane, select the Clear option in the Panes dialog box.

Synchronized scrolling

If you use the Panes command on the Window menu to split your notebook into panes, you can turn synchronized scrolling on or off by clicking the Synchronize option. When the Synchronize option is on, scrolling is simultaneous in both panes. In a horizontally split notebook, the columns scroll together in both panes so that corresponding columns always align; in a vertically split window, the rows scroll together in both panes. When the Synchronize option is off, you can scroll each pane independently.

information. Each row of a database is a record that contains all the pertinent information about one component of the database. For example, row 5 of the invoice log contains all the information about one particular invoice. Each cell of the database is a field that contains one item of information. For example, cell G5 contains the amount of the invoice for the record in row 5. All the fields in a particular column contain the same kind of information about their respective records. For example, column G of the invoice log contains the amounts of all the invoices. At the top of each column is a label, called the field name.

Records

Fields

Field names

In the next sections, we'll cover Quattro Pro's database capabilities. First, however, follow these steps to restore the invoice log to its original order:

1. Make sure only one cell is selected, then choose Sort from the Data menu, and click the Reset button to clear all the fields in the Data Sort dialog box. Type *A5..G48* in the Block edit field, enter a cell reference from column A in the 1st edit field, and click OK. The table is now in its original, unsorted order.

Restoring to original order

2. Delete column A from the notebook page.

Because each field name in a Quattro Pro database should consist of a single word with no spaces, you now need to revise two of the labels at the top of the columns containing invoice data:

1. Select C4, and replace the space between Invoice and Number with an underscore character (_).

2. Select F4, and replace the spaces in this label as well.

Now let's assign a name to the entire database block, including the row of field names. These steps aren't mandatory, but they make searching a database easier.

1. Select A4..F48, and choose Names and then Create from the Block menu.

2. Type the name *inv_db* (for "invoice database") in the Name edit field, and click OK to define the name.

The Database Desktop

The Database Desktop is an external application that allows you to view and edit information in Paradox, dBASE, and SQL files. To start Database Desktop, double-click its icon in the Quattro Pro for Windows group, or choose Database Desktop from the Data menu. Describing all of Database Desktop's functions and features is beyond the scope of this book; see the documentation for details.

3. With A4..F48 still selected, choose the Query command from the Data menu, click Field Names, and then click Close. (This step prepares the database for the operations you'll perform in the next section by creating a series of block names based on the field names and assigning them to the corresponding cells of the first record in the database.)

You are now ready to begin exploring Quattro Pro's database operations, which you perform with the Query command from the Data menu. As you'll see in the following sections, the options in the Data Query dialog box give you a variety of ways to find, delete, and extract database records that match specific criteria you define.

Manipulating Records

Suppose you invested a considerable chunk of your advertising budget for the year on a direct-mail flyer about a two-week promotion. For another two-week promotion earlier in the year, you relied on your salespeople to get the word out to their customers. You want to compare sales during the two promotions. Or suppose you want to analyze all sales over $60,000 to see if you can detect sales patterns. In either case, you can tell Quattro Pro to extract all the relevant invoices for scrutiny.

You give Quattro Pro instructions of this kind by defining criteria in an area of the notebook called the criteria table. For

Mandatory field names

When naming a database block, you must include the field names. If you neglect to include them, Quattro Pro will be unable to perform query operations on the named database.

Field-name conventions

Quattro Pro imposes several rules on the format of field names you create for a database. Each name should consist of a one-word label with no spaces. (Replace spaces in a multi-word field name with underscore characters to make them easier to read in formulas.) The field name must be less than 16 characters long and have no leading or trailing spaces. No two field names can be the same, and a field cannot have the same name as any block in the same notebook.

example, you might tell Quattro Pro to find all the records with amounts over $60,000 by entering >*60000* in the criteria table under the Amount_of_Sale field name.

Creating the Criteria Table

Because Quattro Pro allows you to work with multiple pages in a single notebook, it's a good idea to locate the criteria table on a separate notebook page where it will be easy to find. Later we'll be working with another special area known as the output block, which should also have its own notebook page. Because we'll be working with several notebook pages in this section, we'll refer to blocks and cells by their full references; for example, A:A4..A:F4.

The top row of the criteria table always contains the names of the fields you want to use as criteria for locating records, so start by copying the field names from the database block to the criteria table.

1. Select A:A4..A:F4, and click the Copy button to copy this block of data to the Clipboard.

2. Click the page B tab at the bottom of the notebook window. When page B appears, notice that the cell indicator at the left end of the input line has the page B prefix.

3. Select B:A1, and click the Paste button. Next, select the range B:A1..B:F1, and click the Fit button.

For convenience, you should now assign a name to the criteria table so that you can easily refer to this area in subsequent database operations. Follow these steps:

1. Select B:A1..B:F2, a block that includes the field names and the blank row beneath them where you will enter your criteria.

Assigning names to criteria tables

2. Choose Names and then Create from the Block menu. Notice the names based on the field names that were automatically created when you clicked Field Names in the Data Query dialog box.

3. Type *criteria* in the Name edit field, and click OK to define the name.

Entering Criteria

To have Quattro Pro locate specific records, you enter one or more criteria under the field names in the criteria table. For example, to locate all the invoices for Peter Karnov, you simply enter *Karnov, Peter* under the Salesperson field name in the criteria table. To locate invoices that are both for Peter Karnov *and* have amounts over $10,000—Quattro Pro is to locate records that meet both criteria—you enter *Karnov, Peter* under Salesperson and *>10000* in the same row under Amount_of_Sale. To locate the invoices for Peter Karnov *or* Wally Furban—Quattro Pro is to locate records that meet either of the two criteria—you enter *Karnov, Peter* under the Salesperson field name in the first row and *Furban, Wally* under the Salesperson field name in the next row. (You then need to redefine the criteria table to include three rows.)

Let's try entering criteria that will locate invoices for Peter Karnov with amounts of more than $10,000:

1. In cell B:D2, type *Karnov, Peter*, and press Enter.

2. In cell B:F2, type *+amount_of_sale>10000*, and press Enter. The criteria table looks like this:

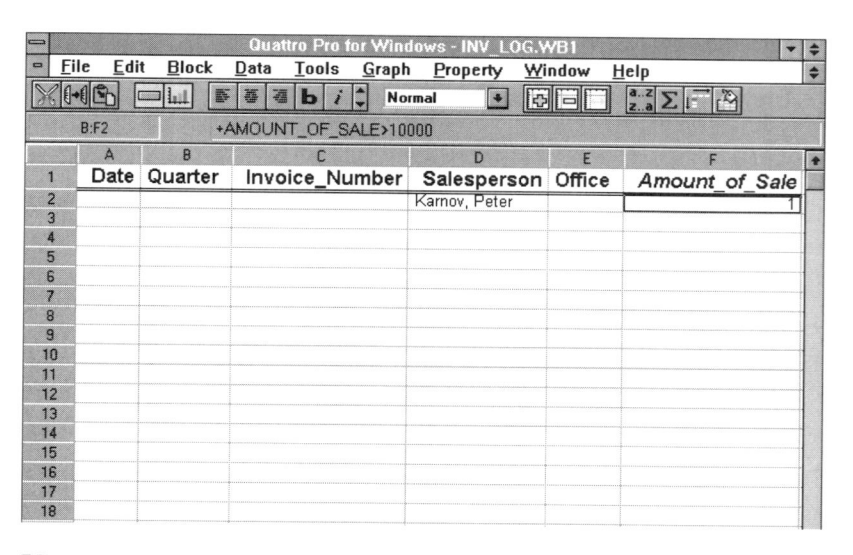

> **Using all field names**
>
> Technically, you could enter only the names of the fields you use as criteria in the criteria table. However, copying all the field names into your criteria table allows you to mix and match criteria as necessary, without having to delete and enter field names each time.

You must now choose Query from the Data menu and tell Quattro Pro whether to locate, delete, or extract the records that match the criteria.

Locating and Deleting Records

Specifying Locate in the Data Query dialog box instructs Quattro Pro to find and highlight the first record in the database that meets the criteria you entered in the criteria table. Let's try this now:

1. Choose Query from the Data menu to display the Data Query dialog box:

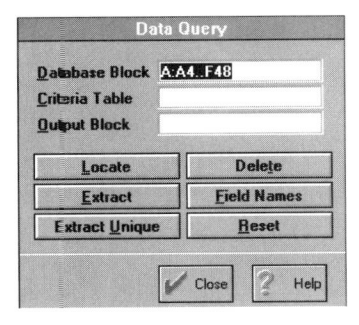

2. Type *inv_db*, the block name of your database, in the Database Block edit field.

3. Type *criteria*, the name of the criteria table, in the Criteria Table edit field. (Don't worry about the Output Block edit field for the moment; it does not apply to a locate operation.)

4. Click Locate. Quattro Pro jumps to the database on page A and highlights the first record that matches the criteria, as shown on the next page. Note the FIND indicator in the status line.

Locating records

No blank rows

You must enter at least one criterion in the criteria table before selecting a query operation in the Data Query dialog box. If you don't, Quattro Pro selects all the records because the blank row does not specify any particular criterion. The presence of blank rows in the criteria table is particularly dangerous when you perform delete operations because all the records will be deleted.

Comparison operators

You can use these comparison operators to compute criteria:

= > < >= <= <>

and you can specify wildcards, using the standard DOS wildcards * and ? for matching text. For example, specifying *Crux,** under Salesperson would locate the records for both Jamie Crux and Tad Crux. Use the tilde character (~) to specify an entry you want to exclude from the selected records.

Only one database

Although you can build several tables of information in the same notebook, only one of them can be designated as the active database at any given time. Quattro Pro recognizes only the block specified in the Database Block edit field of the Query dialog box as the database.

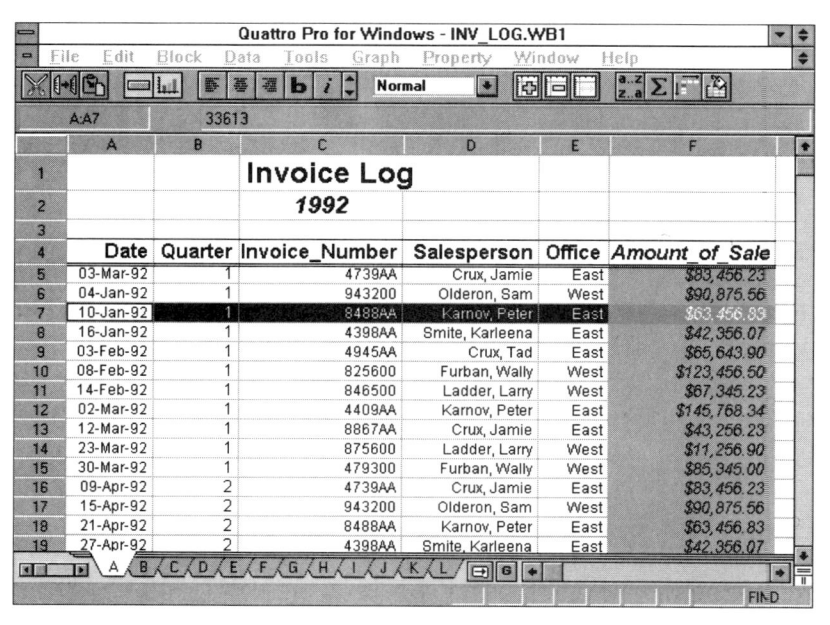

5. Press Down Arrow to move to the next matching record. Continue pressing Down Arrow and viewing additional matching records until the computer beeps to indicate that Quattro Pro has found the last matching record.

6. Now press Up Arrow repeatedly to view previous matching records until the computer beeps.

Exiting FIND mode

7. Press Esc to exit FIND mode. The Data Query dialog box and page B reappear on the screen. Click Close to close the dialog box.

Only one criteria table

Only one block can be designated as the criteria table at any given time. Quattro Pro recognizes only the block specified in the Criteria Table edit field of the Data Query dialog box as the criteria table.

Criteria block names

You can develop different sets of selection criteria in one notebook and assign different block names to each set. In the Criteria Table edit field of the Data Query dialog box, enter the criteria table name that applies to a particular query operation.

Now suppose you want to limit the search to invoices from the first and second quarters of the year. You can press the F7 function key to repeat a query you have already defined in the Data Query dialog box. Try this:

1. Select B:B2 in the criteria table. Type +*quarter<3*, and press Enter.

2. Press the F7 function key to repeat the last locate operation, and then repeatedly press Down Arrow. Quattro Pro now finds only four records.

    Repeating locate operations

3. Press Esc to exit FIND mode and return to page B. (The Data Query dialog box does not reappear on the screen because you initiated this query by pressing F7.)

Specifying Delete in the Data Query dialog box tells Quattro Pro to find and delete the records that meet the criteria in the criteria table. When you click the Delete button, Quattro Pro displays a message box asking you to confirm that you want to delete the matching records. Click Yes to proceed with the deletion, or click No if you first want to check that the criteria you have entered won't cause Quattro Pro to delete records you really need to keep. It's always a good idea to perform a locate operation with a newly developed set of criteria so that you can examine the records that match the criteria before you delete them.

Deleting records

Logical operators

You can use Quattro Pro's logical operators—#AND#, #OR#, and #NOT#—in criteria formulas. For example, entering the following formula in the Amount_of_Sale field in the criteria table instructs Quattro Pro to look for all records in which the amount is greater than $50,000 and less than $150,000:

+AMOUNT>50000#AND#
  AMOUNT<150000

Criteria in the same field

To locate records using two criteria in the same field, you must add a second field with the same field name to the criteria table. For example, to locate invoices from the second *or* third quarter, you would add a second Quarter field name in row 1, reset the criteria table, and enter +*Quarter>1* under one Quarter field name and +*Quarter<4* under the other Quarter field name.

Extracting Records

Specifying Extract in the Data Query dialog box tells Quattro Pro to find and copy the records that meet the criteria into an area of the notebook called the output block. Before initiating an extraction, you must create the output block so that Quattro Pro knows where to put the records. The procedure for creating the output block is almost identical to the procedure for creating the criteria table. Follow these steps to create an output block on page C of INV_LOG.WB1:

1. Select B:A1..B:F1, and click the Copy button.

2. Click the page C tab, check that C:A1 is selected, and click the Paste button.

3. Select C:A1..C:F1, and click the Fit button.

Defining the ouput block

4. With C:A1..C:F1 still selected, choose Names and then Create from the Block menu, type *output* as the name of the output block, and click OK.

Now you can tell Quattro Pro to extract the records that meet the criteria in the criteria table:

1. Select B:B2, and press the Delete key to delete the quarter criterion you entered in the previous example.

2. Choose Query from the Data menu. In the Data Query dialog box, click the Output Block edit field, and press the F3 function key to display the Block Names dialog box. Select OUTPUT, and click OK to close the dialog box and insert that name in the Output Block edit field.

Output-block field names

As with the criteria table, the top row of the output block must contain field names. If you include only some of the fields, Quattro Pro extracts only those fields from the database.

3. Back at the Data Query dialog box, click the Extract button, and then click Close to close the dialog box.

4. Click the page C tab to move to that page. Here are the results (we've adjusted column widths and formatted column A to display dates and column F to display currency):

Chapter 3 Extracting Information from a Database

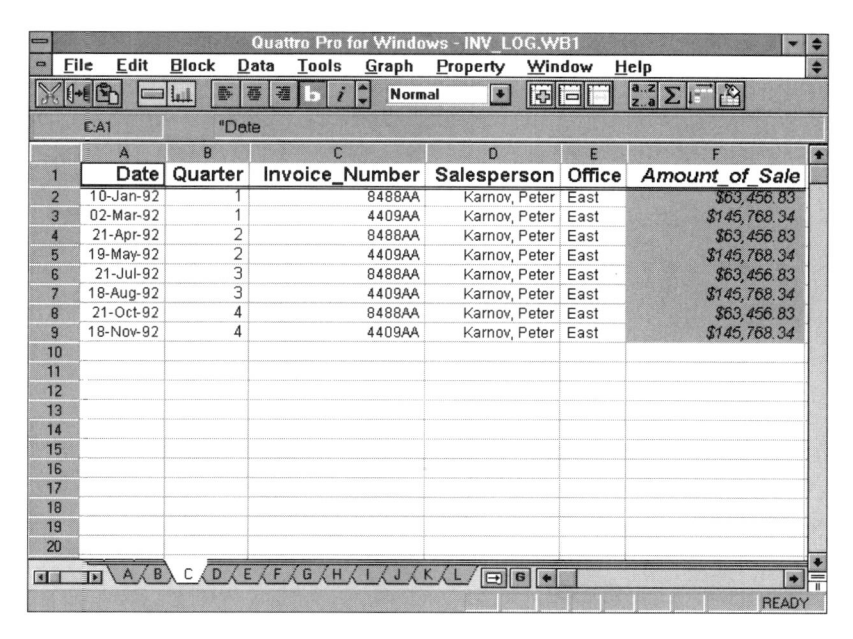

[Screenshot of Quattro Pro for Windows - INV_LOG.WB1 showing the following data:]

	Date	Quarter	Invoice_Number	Salesperson	Office	Amount_of_Sale
2	10-Jan-92	1	8488AA	Karnov, Peter	East	$63,456.83
3	02-Mar-92	1	4409AA	Karnov, Peter	East	$145,768.34
4	21-Apr-92	2	8488AA	Karnov, Peter	East	$63,456.83
5	19-May-92	2	4409AA	Karnov, Peter	East	$145,768.34
6	21-Jul-92	3	8488AA	Karnov, Peter	East	$63,456.83
7	18-Aug-92	3	4409AA	Karnov, Peter	East	$145,768.34
8	21-Oct-92	4	8488AA	Karnov, Peter	East	$63,456.83
9	18-Nov-92	4	4409AA	Karnov, Peter	East	$145,768.34

Before we move on, take a moment to name your three notebook pages and save your work:

1. Right-click the page A tab to open the page Object Inspector. In the Page Name edit field, type *LOG*, and click OK. The label LOG replaces the letter A on the page tab. Changing page names in this manner makes it much easier to navigate through notebooks. Notice that the name also replaces the letter A in the cell indicator. You can use either the page name or its letter in formulas.

Extracting unique records

Clicking the Extract Unique button in the Data Query dialog box tells Quattro Pro to extract only one instance of repeated records. This helps manage output blocks for databases with many redundant entries.

Preserving extracted records

When you extract database records, Quattro Pro overwrites any previously extracted records in the output block. If you want to preserve the records, you must either move them or create a new output block for the next extract operation.

2. Repeat step 1 for pages B and C, naming them CRIT and OUT, repectively. (Page names must be different from block names; otherwise, formulas and database query operations may produce erroneous results.)

3. Choose Save from the File menu.

   This discussion of databases has necessarily been brief, but you should now know enough to explore various ways of manipulating your own data using criteria and the Data Query dialog box.

Using Group Mode

Suppose you want to use the information in INV_LOG.WB1 to analyze the performance of your salespeople. You want to create identical notebook pages for each person—that's seven notebook pages to set up before you can get going with the analysis. In this section, we'll demonstrate how you can use groups of pages to reduce that setup time.

Groups consist of notebook pages that you temporarily link together so that any editing or formatting you do on one page is applied to the other pages. Let's take a closer look. To make it easier for you to follow along, we'll work with only two notebook pages, but you can create as many as you need.

1. Choose New from the File menu to create a new notebook, and save it as REVIEWS.WB1.

Moving pages

Once you've set up several pages in a notebook, you might want to move a page to another location in the notebook. Simply drag the page tab down to the status line and then to its new position in the page tab line-up. When you release the mouse button, the surrounding pages either move back one page or forward one page, depending on which way you moved the page tab. Surrounding pages change letters to remain in alphabetical order (except for named pages). For example, if you move page D in front of the Criteria page, it becomes page A, and the former page E becomes page D.

2. Right-click the page A tab, and name it *Template*. Then name page B *Karnov_P*. (You must use underscores instead of commas and spaces in page names.) Name page C *Furban_W*.

3. To group these three pages, click the tab for the first page. Then hold down Shift, and click the tab for the third page. Quattro Pro draws a black line below the three page tabs to indicate that they are selected.

Designating group members

4. Choose Define Group from the Tools menu to display this dialog box:

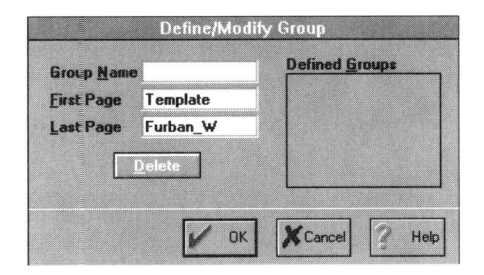

5. Type *Employees* in the Group Name edit field, and click OK.

Defining groups

Now that you've defined the group, let's turn on Group mode and make some entries:

1. Click the Group button at the bottom of the notebook window (the one with a *G* on it). The line under the group page tabs turns blue, indicating that you are in Group mode.

Turning on Group mode

2. Select TEMPLATE:A1, and make the following entries in the new notebook, pressing Ctrl-Enter after each entry instead of pressing Enter or clicking the ✓ box:

TEMPLATE:A1	SALES PERFORMANCE, 1992
TEMPLATE:A3	Name
TEMPLATE:A4	Total Sales
TEMPLATE:A5	Number of Sales
TEMPLATE:A6	Average Sale
TEMPLATE:A7	Largest Sale
TEMPLATE:A8	Smallest Sale
TEMPLATE:A9	Contribution to Total Sales

3. Select TEMPLATE:A1..TEMPLATE:A9, and click the Bold button on the SpeedBar.

4. Widen column A so that all the entries fit within the column.

5. Now flip between the group pages, noting that Quattro Pro has made all entries and formatting in all three pages.

6. Move back to the *TEMPLATE* page, and make B3 bold. Then format B4 and B6..B8 with the Currency style, and format *B9* with the Percent style.

Exiting Group mode

7. Click the Group button to turn off Group mode, and then save the REVIEWS.WB1 notebook.

Using Database @Functions

Quattro Pro offers a small but important group of special-purpose @functions designed to calculate statistical values from selected records in a database. To distinguish these @functions from regular notebook @functions, the names of the database @functions begin with @D. For example, given a selection of records, @DSUM finds the total of the values in a particular numeric field. Likewise, @DAVG calculates an average, @DMIN and @DMAX find the smallest and largest entries, and @DCOUNT determines the number of entries in the selection of records. We'll experiment with all five of these @functions in this section.

It's important to understand the difference between the database @functions and their equivalent notebook @functions. A notebook function typically operates on all the values in the block supplied as the function's argument, whereas a database function begins by selecting the records on which it will perform its calculation. For this reason, the database @functions include arguments that specify the location of the database, the field in which the calculation will be performed, and the location of a criteria table that Quattro Pro can use to determine which records to include in the calculation.

For example, in a minute you'll use this function in the REVIEWS.WB1 notebook:

@DSUM([INV_LOG]INV_DB,5,[INV_LOG]CRITERIA)

The function's first argument, [INV_LOG]INV_DB, is an external reference to the invoice database. The [INV_LOG] part of the argument tells Quattro Pro the name of the notebook that contains the records to be used in the formula, and

---

Returning to a group

Quattro Pro remembers which notebook pages were part of your last group. If you disband the group by turning off Group mode, you can return to the group by clicking the Group button again.

Chapter 3 Extracting Information from a Database

INV_DB is the name assigned to the database itself. The second argument is the number of the column that contains the field you want Quattro Pro to total with the @DSUM function. (Quattro Pro starts numbering columns from 0, so the Amount_of_Sale column is 5.) The third argument, [INV_LOG]CRITERIA, is an external reference to the criteria table in which you have entered one or more criteria that determine the records to be selected.

In this section, we're going to use several database @functions to perform calculations on the sales made by Peter Karnov and Wally Furban. Instead of having to copy the invoice information to the pages we just created for these two salespeople, we can tell Quattro Pro to select their records from the INV_LOG notebook, perform the calculations, and put the results in the REVIEWS notebook. We'll start by telling Quattro Pro which records to use:

1. From the Window menu, choose INV_LOG.WB1.

2. Click the CRIT page tab, delete the criterion in F2, and leave *Karnov, Peter* in D2 (under the Salesperson column).

3. Return to REVIEWS.WB1 by choosing it from the bottom of the Window menu.

Now you're ready to begin entering formulas in the REVIEWS notebook to calculate sales statistics for the selected salesperson. By carefully designing all the formulas, you'll be able to use them to create a profile for any salesperson. As you'll see in a moment, Quattro Pro's database @functions are very flexible. All you'll have to do to create a new profile is change the name in cell CRIT:D2 of the criteria table. Let's get going:

1. Make the following entries in the indicated cells (type them without any line breaks or spaces):

    TEMPLATE:B3   +[INV_LOG]CRIT:D2
    TEMPLATE:B4   @DSUM([INV_LOG]INV_DB,5,
                   [INV_LOG]CRITERIA)
    TEMPLATE:B5   @DCOUNT([INV_LOG]INV_DB,5,
                   [INV_LOG]CRITERIA)
    TEMPLATE:B6   @DAVG([INV_LOG]INV_DB,5,
                   [INV_LOG]CRITERIA)

External references

A quick way to insert an external reference in a formula is to use POINT mode. First check that the external notebook is open. Then when you need to enter the external reference in the formula, choose the external notebook from the Window menu, select the block you want to reference, and type any necessary commas or closing parentheses. When you enter the formula, you return to the original notebook.

TEMPLATE:B7	@DMAX([INV_LOG]INV_DB,5, [INV_LOG]CRITERIA)
TEMPLATE:B8	@DMIN([INV_LOG]INV_DB,5, [INV_LOG]CRITERIA)
TEMPLATE:B9	+B4/[INV_LOG]INV:F49

Adjusting columns in group notebooks

2. You need to widen column B so that the numeric values can be displayed properly. Widen this column in all the pages in the Employees group by clicking the Group button and then widening column B. Then click the Group button again to turn off Group mode. Here is the result of your work at this point:

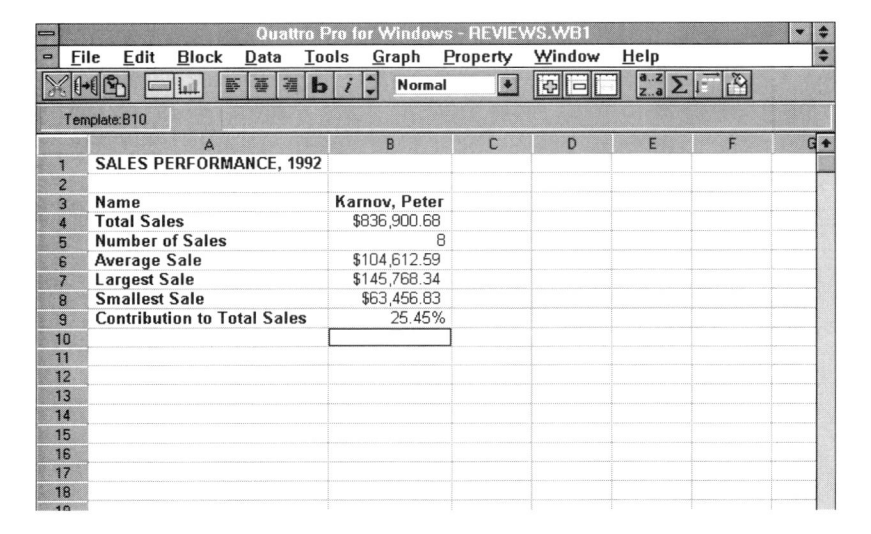

As you can see, each of the database @functions has selected all the invoice records for Peter Karnov and performed a statistical calculation on the values in the Amount_of_Sale column of the selected records. Changing the name of the salesperson in the criteria table of INV_LOG.WB1 will automatically change the data on the TEMPLATE page of the REVIEWS.WB1 notebook, creating the profile for that salesperson. To preserve the profile for Peter Karnov, you need to move his data to the appropriate page, like this:

1. Copy the TEMPLATE:B3..B9 block, and click the page tab for KARNOV_P.

Pasting values only

2. Select B3 on this page, and choose Paste Special from the Edit menu. In the Paste Special dialog box, select the Values Only option, and click OK. Quattro Pro pastes only the values, not the underlying formulas, into cells B3..B9.

Suppose you now want to view the sales profile for Wally Furban. Here are the steps:

1. Choose INV_LOG.WB1 from the Window menu, and change the entry in cell CRIT:D2 to *Furban, Wally*.

2. Choose REVIEWS.WB1 from the Window menu, and click the TEMPLATE page tab. Quattro Pro has recalculated the formulas using Wally Furban's records instead of Peter Karnov's.

3. Copy TEMPLATE:B3..B9, and use the Values Only option of the Paste Special command to copy the profile to the FURBAN_W page. Here's the result:

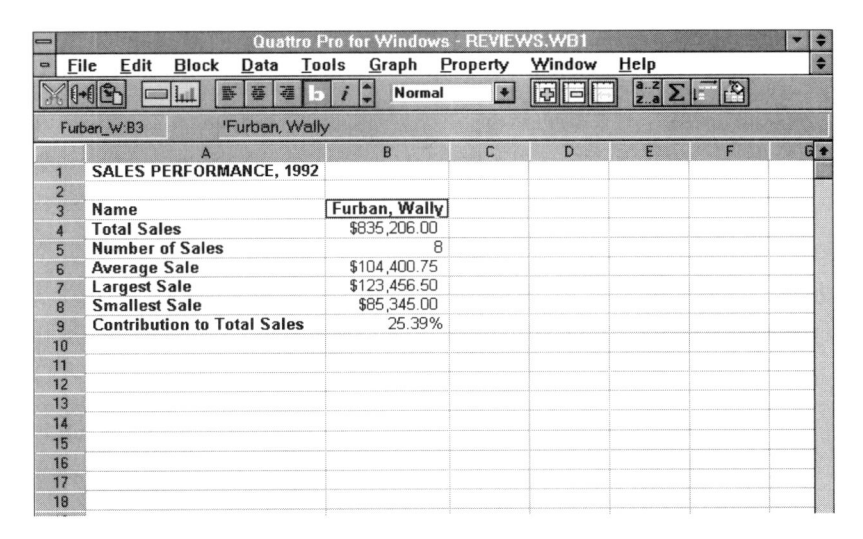

	A	B
1	SALES PERFORMANCE, 1992	
3	Name	Furban, Wally
4	Total Sales	$835,206.00
5	Number of Sales	8
6	Average Sale	$104,400.75
7	Largest Sale	$123,456.50
8	Smallest Sale	$85,345.00
9	Contribution to Total Sales	25.39%

4. Choose the Save All command from the File menu to save both the INV_LOG and REVIEWS notebooks.

Clearly, the database @functions are powerful tools to have at your disposal as you create and work with your own databases in Quattro Pro. We'll leave you to experiment with the linking formulas you have created on the Template page of the REVIEWS notebook. For example, you might try changing some of the sales amounts in the INV_LOG database to see the effect on the sales profiles. Or you might want to further refine the analysis by breaking down the sales for each salesperson by quarter, in which case you would add a second criterion in the Quarter column of the criteria table in INV_LOG.WB1.

Saving all notebooks

Hotlinks

When you open a notebook with references to cells in a closed notebook, Quattro Pro displays the Hotlinks dialog box and asks whether you want to open the supporting notebook, update the link without opening the supporting notebook, or do neither. You can also use the Update Links command on the Tools menu to open, refresh, delete, and change links.

4
Tracking Budgets

Setting Up the Budget 90
Working with Graphs in the Notebook Environment 92
Changing the Graph Type 94
Formatting Notebook Graphs 98
Working with Graphs in the Graph Environment 102
Creating Picture Graphs 105
Printing Graphs 107

Creating graphs
Page 92

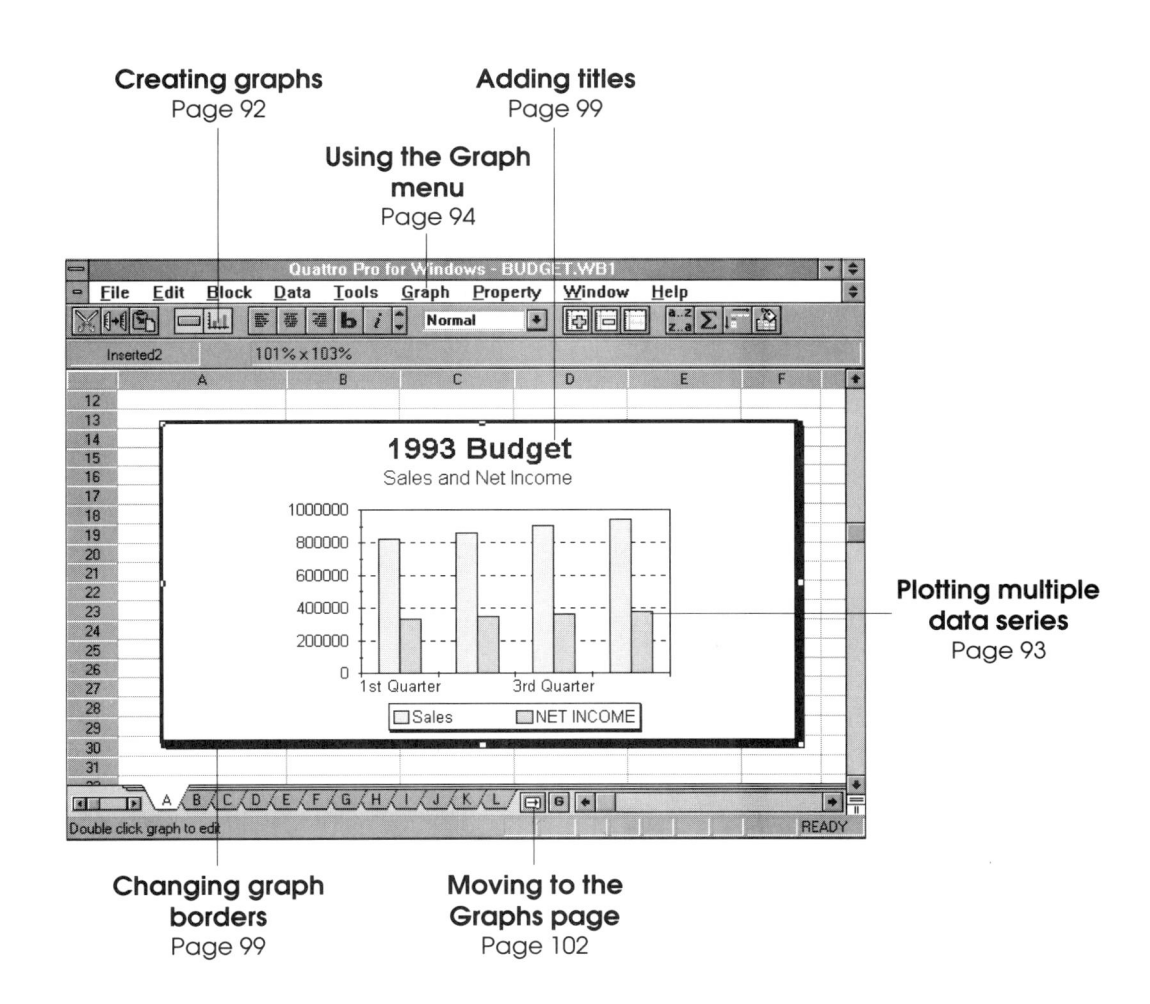

Adding titles
Page 99

Using the Graph menu
Page 94

Plotting multiple data series
Page 93

Changing graph borders
Page 99

Moving to the Graphs page
Page 102

In the previous chapters, you learned a lot about Quattro Pro, and you now know enough to put Quattro Pro to use in your own business environment. After all that hard work, let's relax a bit. Using a budget notebook as a basis, in this chapter we explore the various ways you can visually present notebook data.

Setting Up the Budget

We'll start by showing you step by step how to set up this projected budget notebook:

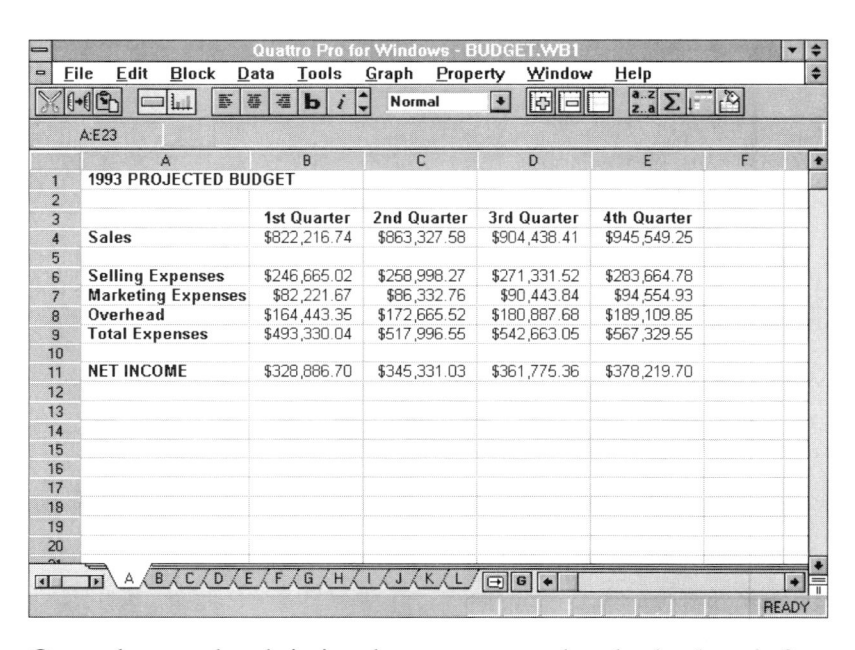

Once the notebook is in place, we can plot the budget information as various kinds of graphs. Assuming that Quattro Pro is loaded, follow these steps to create the notebook:

1. If you don't have a new, blank notebook on your screen, save and close any open notebooks, and choose New from the File menu.

2. Save the notebook as BUDGET.WB1.

3. In cell A1, type *'1993 PROJECTED BUDGET* as the notebook title, click the ✓ button, and then make the title bold.

4. In cell B3, type ^*1st Quarter*, and press Right Arrow to enter the label and select cell C3. Then enter ^*2nd Quarter*, ^*3rd Quarter*, and ^*4th Quarter* in cells C3..E3.

Chapter 4 Tracking Budgets   91

5. Select B3..E3, click the ✓ button, and then click the Fit button.

6. In cell A4, type *Sales*, and click the ✓ button.

7. Next, enter these sales amounts in the indicated cells:

B4	822216.74
C4	863327.58
D4	904438.41
E4	945549.25

Now let's tackle the expenses. For this example, assume that we have selling expenses that average 30 percent of sales, marketing expenses that average 10 percent, and overhead expenses (fixed costs) that average 20 percent.

1. Enter the following information in the indicated cells:

A6	Selling Expenses
A7	Marketing Expenses
A8	Overhead
A9	Total Expenses
B6	0.3*B4
B7	0.1*B4
B8	0.2*B4
B9	@SUM(B6..B8)

2. Select B6..B9, and click the Copy button. Then select C6..E9, and click Paste to duplicate the 1st Quarter formulas for the 2nd, 3rd, and 4th Quarters.

3. Select B4..E11, and then select Currency from the Style list on the SpeedBar.

4. Select A4..A11, click the Bold button, and then click the Fit button.

Finally, let's compute the net income:

1. In cell A11, type *NET INCOME*, and press Right Arrow to enter the label and select B11.

2. With B11 selected, type *+B4–B9*, and click the ✓ button. Quattro Pro enters the result, $328,886.70, as the 1st Quarter's net income.

3. Copy the formula in cell B11, and paste it into cells C11..E11.

Voilà! Your budget notebook should now look like the one shown on page 90.

Working with Graphs in the Notebook Environment

With Quattro Pro, you can create graphs in two ways: as a floating graphic on the notebook page or separately in a graph window. In this section, we show you how to quickly plot data as a floating graphic. The advantage of this method is that you can print the graph and the underlying notebook on one sheet of paper. We'll create the graph using the Graph tool on the SpeedBar. The Graph tool automates the otherwise complex process of creating and then formatting notebook graphs.

Follow these steps to create a bar graph from the expense data in BUDGET.WB1:

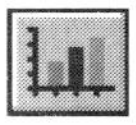

Creating graphs

1. Select A3..E4, and click the Graph tool.

2. Move the pointer to the blank area below your notebook entries, hold down the mouse button, and drag to create a frame about the size of the notebook window. Then release the mouse button. Quattro Pro displays the graph shown here:

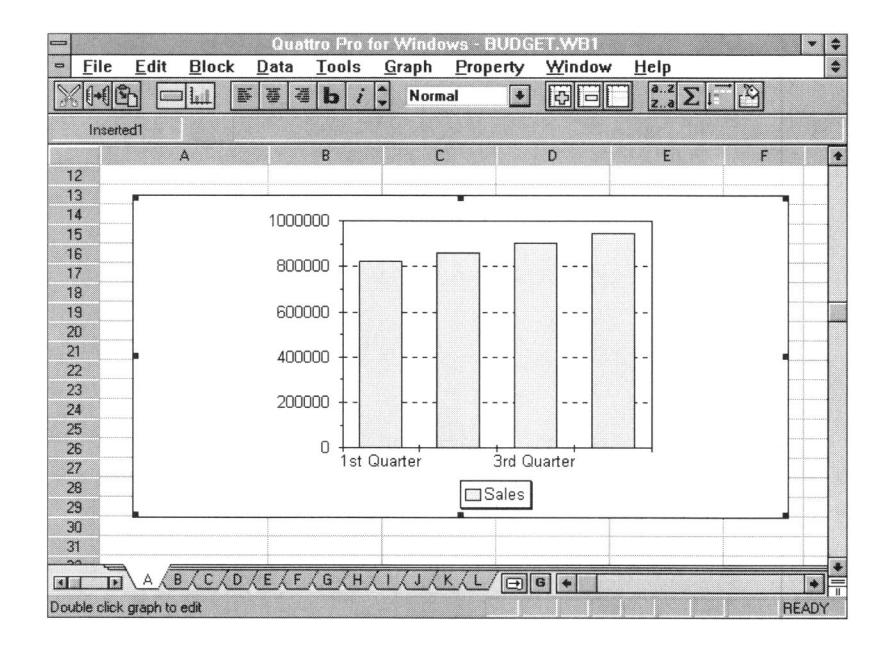

Quattro Pro has drawn a bar graph of the data in A3..E4, with the 1st and 3rd Quarter labels along the x-axis (the horizontal axis) and dollar amounts at regular intervals along the y-axis (the vertical axis). When you create a new graph from a notebook block, Quattro Pro begins by depicting your data as a bar graph. The label from cell A4, Sales, has been used as the graph's legend.

We have plotted only one set of data, called a data series. Let's see what the graph looks like when we plot two series:

1. The single-series notebook graph should be active. (Black squares, called handles, appear around the graph's perimeter to indicate that it is active.) If it isn't, simply click it. ⟵ **Active graph**

2. Press the Delete key to delete the graph from the notebook page. (Although you delete it from the page, Quattro Pro retains it in memory until you delete it from the Graphs page, which we discuss later.) ⟵ **Deleting graphs**

3. Select the series in A3..E4 again. Then select a second series by holding down the Ctrl key and selecting A11..E11. ⟵ **Plotting multiple data series**

4. Click the Graph tool, and drag another frame in the blank area below the notebook entries. Quattro Pro displays the selected data in its default two-dimensional bar graph format, with a legend:

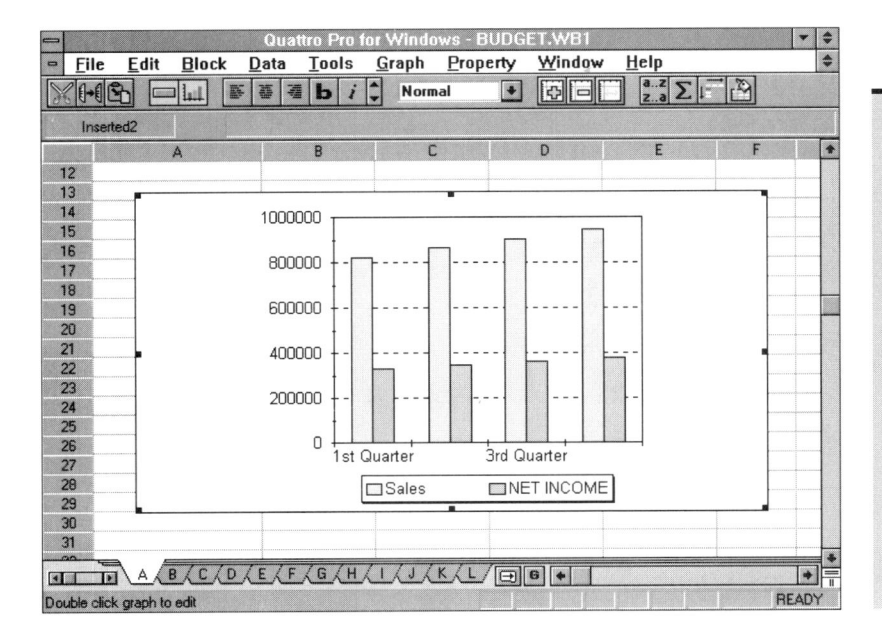

Graph labels

If you include column or row labels when selecting the data you want Quattro Pro to graph, Quattro Pro uses them as axis labels, whether you are creating a floating graph or a graph in a graph window.

The sales amounts and net-income amounts are grouped in quarters and are represented by columns of different colors or shades, which are identified in the legend.

Automatic updating

Notebook graphs are actively linked to the data Quattro Pro uses to plot them, and they automatically change if the data changes. Try this:

1. Change one of the sales amounts in B4..E4. The Sales column grows or shrinks to reflect the change.

2. Choose Undo Entry from the Edit menu to undo the change.

Changing the Graph Type

As you have just seen, creating notebook graphs is very easy. You simply select the data, click the Graph tool, and create the graph frame. Quattro Pro fills in all the details. If you want to format this graph or change it to a different type, you can use the commands on the Graph menu or you can open the graph in a graph window. We'll show you how to use the Graph menu first.

1. Check that the notebook graph is selected.

Using the Graph menu

2. Choose Type from the Graph menu. Quattro Pro displays this dialog box:

Graph scale

If you change the source data radically, the scale of the entire graph can change. For example, if you enter a sales amount in the millions in BUDGET.WB1, the other columns shrink down to almost nothing to keep the scale consistent.

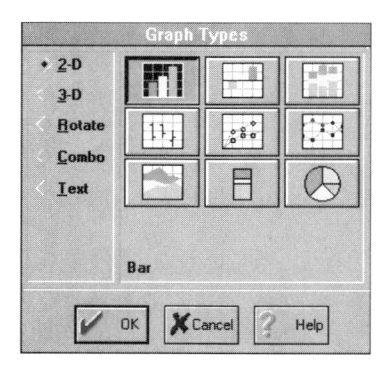

Quattro Pro offers the following types of graphs:

- Bar graphs, which are great for showing the values of several items at a single point in time.

- Line graphs, which are often used to show variations in the value of more than one item over time.

- Stack bar and area graphs, which plot multiple data series as cumulative layers, showing the relationship of values to a total.
- Pie and column graphs, which are ideal for showing the percentages of an item that can be assigned to the item's components.
- XY (or scatter) graphs, which are used to detect correlations between independent items (such as a person's height and weight).
- High-low graphs, which illustrate the difference between corresponding values in two series.
- Surface graphs, which plot columns and rows as intersecting lines on a three-dimensional surface.

In addition, you can create various kinds of combination graphs, which plot one type of graph on top of another as an "overlay." ← **Combination graphs**

Quattro Pro divides these graph types into five categories: 2-D, 3-D, Rotate, Combo, and Text. Each category offers several variations of the basic chart types. This array of possibilities will probably satisfy most of your graphing needs.

Let's try changing the type of the graph currently on your screen so that you can see some of the possibilities.

Graph menu

The Graph menu contains several commands for creating and formatting graphs. New lets you create a graph by selecting data series one at a time. Edit allows you to select a graph to edit from a list. Insert and Delete list all graphs in a notebook and allow you to insert a graph on a specific notebook page or delete a graph from the notebook. Copy allows you to copy graph styles, data, or annotated objects from one graph to another. View displays the selected graph as it will appear in a Slide Show—in full-page view. (See the tip about the Graphs Page SpeedBar on page 104 for more information.)

Moving and sizing

You can move a notebook graph anywhere on the screen by dragging it, and you can make it larger or smaller by dragging one of the black handles around its frame in the direction in which you want the frame to grow.

Rotating graphs

1. Click the Rotate category. The top-left graph type is selected by default, so simply click OK to change to this graph type. Quattro Pro reorients the bar graph so that the data is presented horizontally. Notice that the figures along the x-axis now appear garbled.

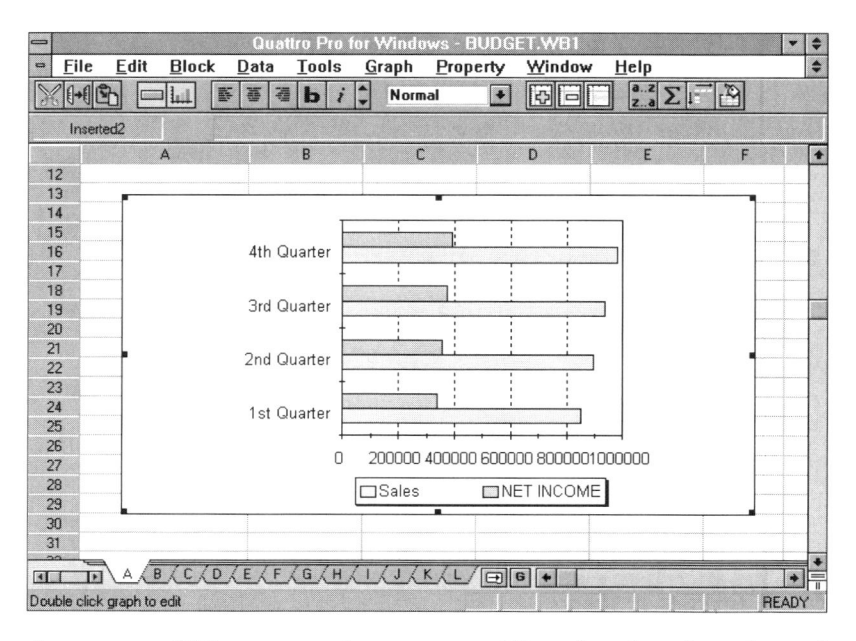

As you try different graph types, you'll notice that the selected data doesn't format well (or at all) in some types. For example, both the 2-D and the 3-D pie formats display only one data series. To display several series using pie graphs, you must use one of the multiple pie graphs in the Combo category.

Underlying values

The format of the values in your notebook does not affect the way they are plotted. Quattro Pro always uses the underlying values when plotting graphs.

Text graphs

Clicking the Text property in the Graph Types dialog box creates a blank graph to which you can add graphics and text boxes in a graph window. You can also create a text graph by choosing New from the Graph menu or, when the Graphs page is active, by clicking the Graph tool on the SpeedBar. In the blank graph, you can then use the drawing tools on the Graph SpeedBar to draw lines, shapes, and arrows in a variety of colors and patterns. You can also type text in text boxes and apply a wide range of formats. For even fancier effects, you can import text and graphics from other Windows applications via the Clipboard.

2. Choose Types again. This time click the Combo option, select the bottom-right graph, and click OK. As shown here, Quattro Pro redisplays the graph as two separate 3-D pies.

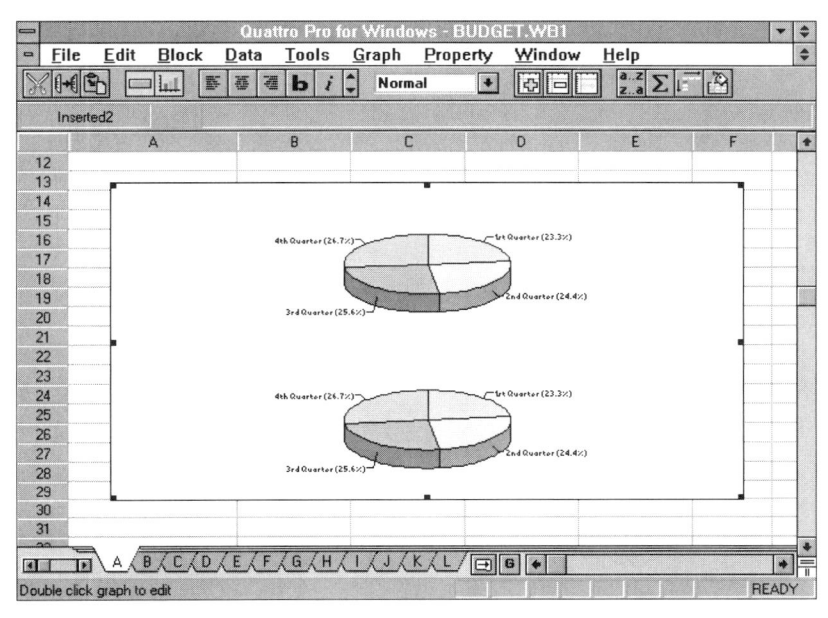

3. In the 2-D category of the Graph Types dialog box, select the second graph in the second line, and click OK. Quattro Pro draws this line graph:

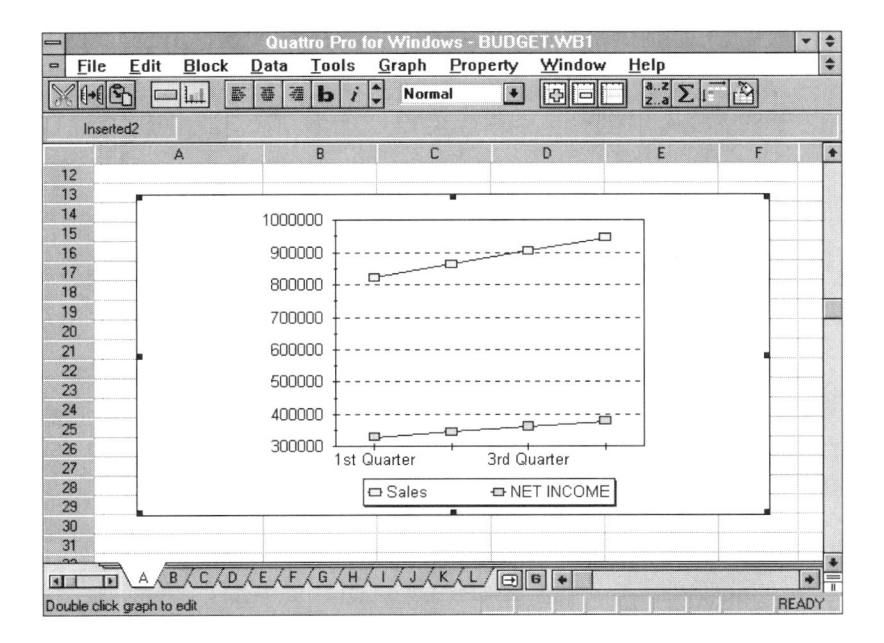

4. Now change the graph to a 3-D bar graph by selecting the top-left graph in the 3-D category of the Graph Types dialog box. Here's the result.

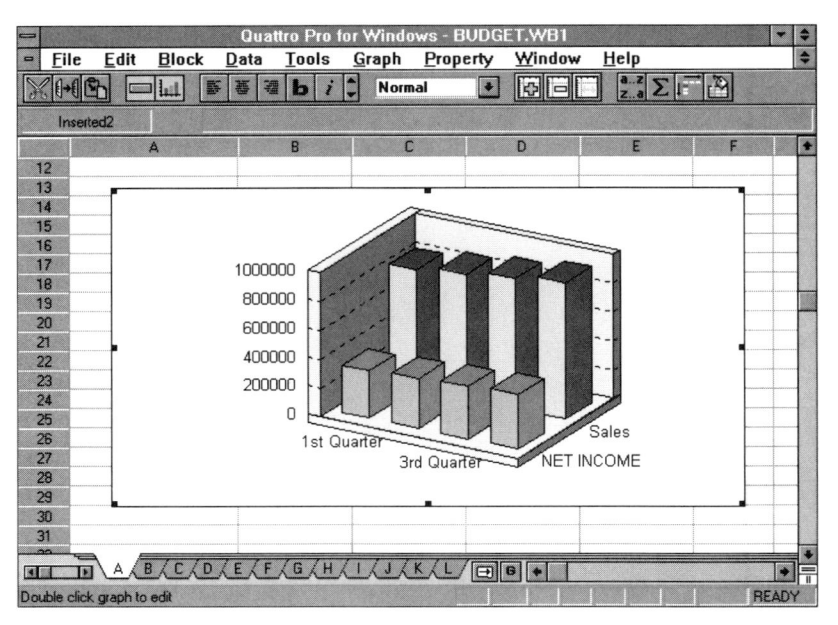

5. Return to the original version of the graph by selecting the first graph type in the 2-D category.

6. Save the notebook before proceeding.

   You might want to spend some time familiarizing yourself with the other predefined graph types so that you have an idea of what's available.

Formatting Notebook Graphs

In addition to changing graph types, you can use the commands on the Graph menu, as well as the graph Object Inspector, to format graphs. Here's how:

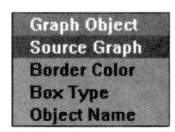

1. First right-click the graph to display the graph Object Inspector menu. Among other things, this menu allows you to change the graph's border thickness and color.

Chapter 4 Tracking Budgets

2. Choose Box Type to display this dialog box:

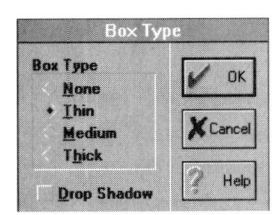

3. Select the Medium and Drop Shadow options, and then click OK. Quattro Pro redraws the graph border, like this:

Changing graph borders

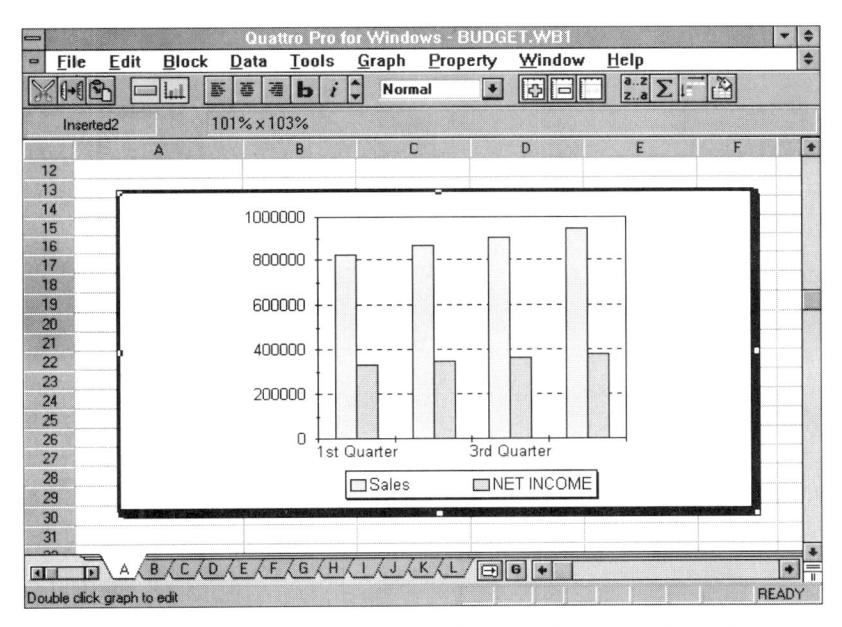

4. From the Graph menu, choose Titles. Quattro Pro displays this dialog box:

Adding titles

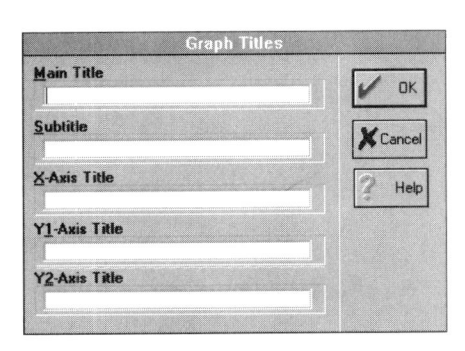

The five edit fields in the dialog box allow you to create two graph titles and three axis labels.

5. Enter *1993 Budget* in the Main Title edit field and *Sales and Net Income* in the Subtitle edit field. Then click OK. Now the graph looks like this:

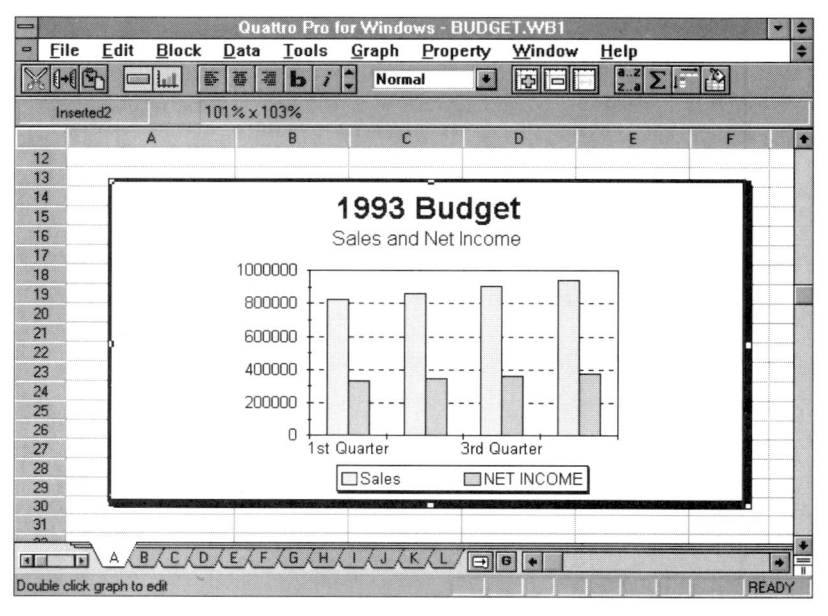

Adding data series

6. Next, choose Series from the Graph menu to display the Graph Series dialog box:

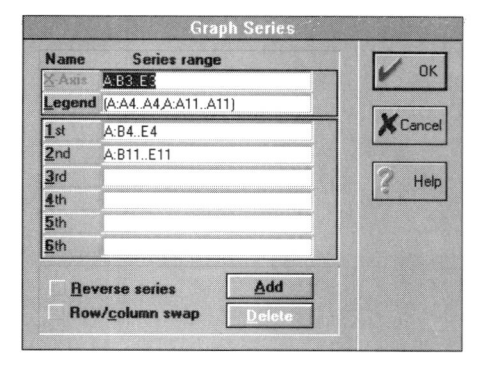

You use this dialog box to make adjustments to the blocks Quattro Pro is using to draw the current graph. As you can see, Quattro Pro initially uses the labels in B3..E3 as the x-axis labels and the labels in A4 and A11 as the legend labels. The block references in the 1st and 2nd edit fields are the data series Quattro Pro actually plots on the graph. To add another data series to the graph, you can click one of the buttons next to the Series Range fields and select the block containing the series on the notebook page.

7. Select the Row/Column Swap option, and click OK. Quattro Pro redraws the graph using the information that appears in columns in the notebook as data series and swapping the x-axis and legend labels, as shown here:

A different view of the data

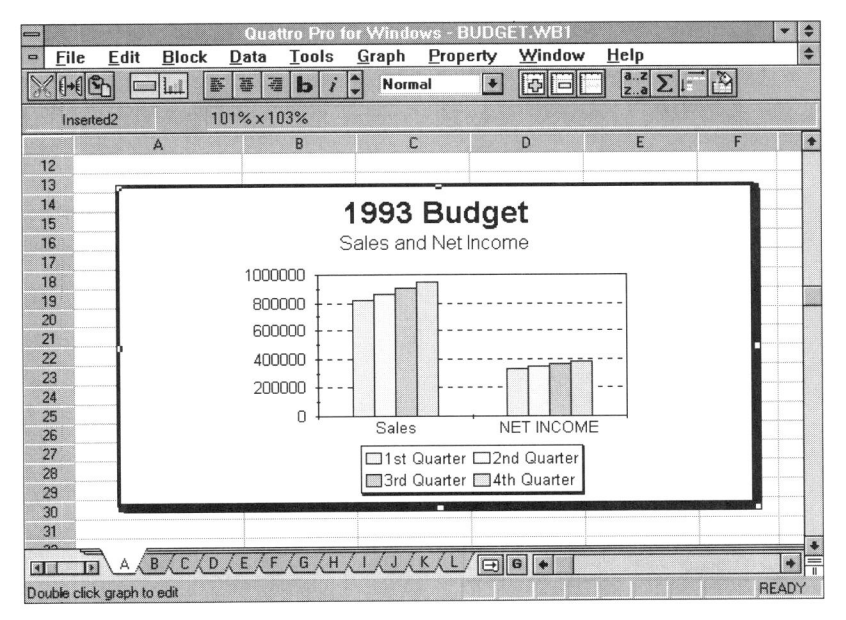

8. Choose Undo Series Apply from the Edit menu to revert to the original graph.

Big graphs

A graph in a graph window can be only as large as the screen. However, you can make a notebook graph very large because you can scroll the graph frame beyond the edge of the screen. Practical uses of this undocumented feature might be limited, but it's fun to play with!

Copying graphs

To cut or copy a graph from one notebook page to another, select the graph, choose Cut or Copy, flip to the destination page, and choose Paste. To copy a graph from the Graphs page, select the graph's icon, choose Copy, move to the destination page, and then choose Paste.

Working with Graphs in the Graph Environment

So far, we have created a notebook graph and applied some rudimentary formatting to it. To apply more sophisticated formatting, you can open the graph in its own window. There, you can use the Graph SpeedBar and the graph Object Inspectors to change almost any aspect of the graph.

When you deleted the first graph you created, we mentioned that Quattro Pro retains the graph in memory. Let's use that graph in this section to demonstrate some more formatting techniques.

Moving to the Graphs page

1. Click the SpeedTab button at the bottom of the notebook page. Quattro Pro flips to the Graphs page, where it displays an icon for each of the graphs you created in the notebook, as well as the Graphs Page SpeedBar.

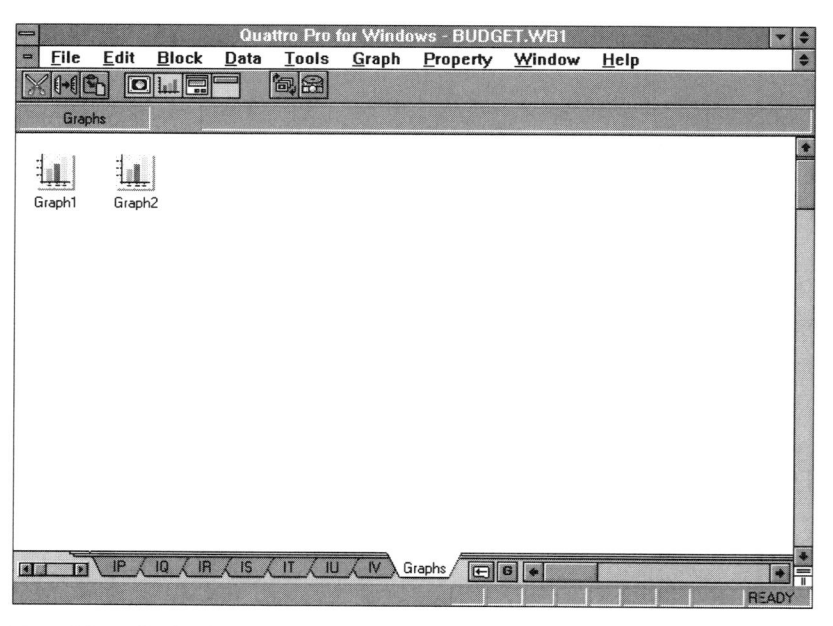

Opening a graph window

2. Double-click the Graph1 icon. Quattro Pro opens the graph in its own window, displays the Graph SpeedBar, and adds a new menu, Draw, to the menu bar.

Chapter 4 Tracking Budgets

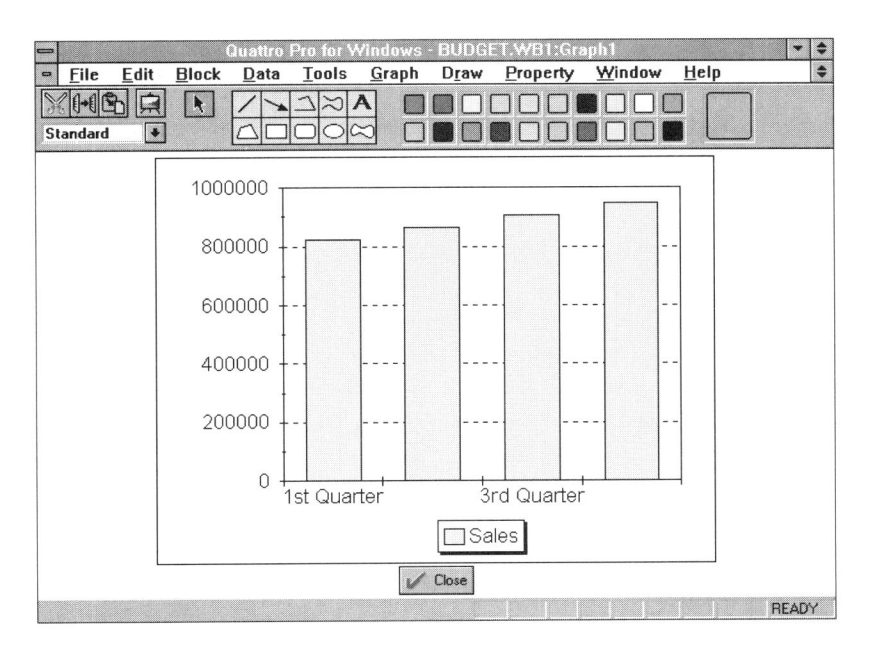

You can right-click any object in the graph window to display its Object Inspector. You can also use the commands on the Property menu to open the various graph Object Inspectors.

1. Right-click one of the numbers on the y-axis to open this y-axis Object Inspector.

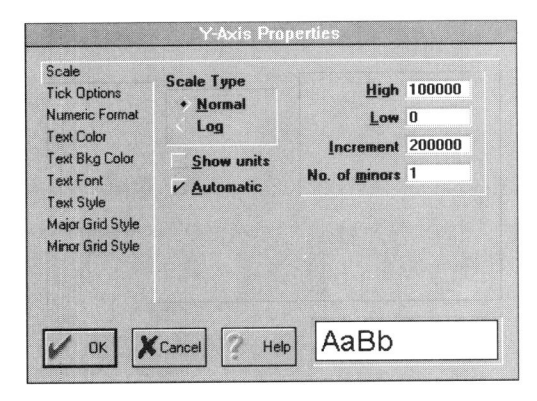

2. Click a few properties in the Object Inspector to view the different formatting possibilities. Then select the Numeric Format property, select the Currency format, enter 0 as the number of decimal places, and click OK. Quattro Pro formats the y-axis numbers as dollars and cents, making them easier to read, as shown on the next page.

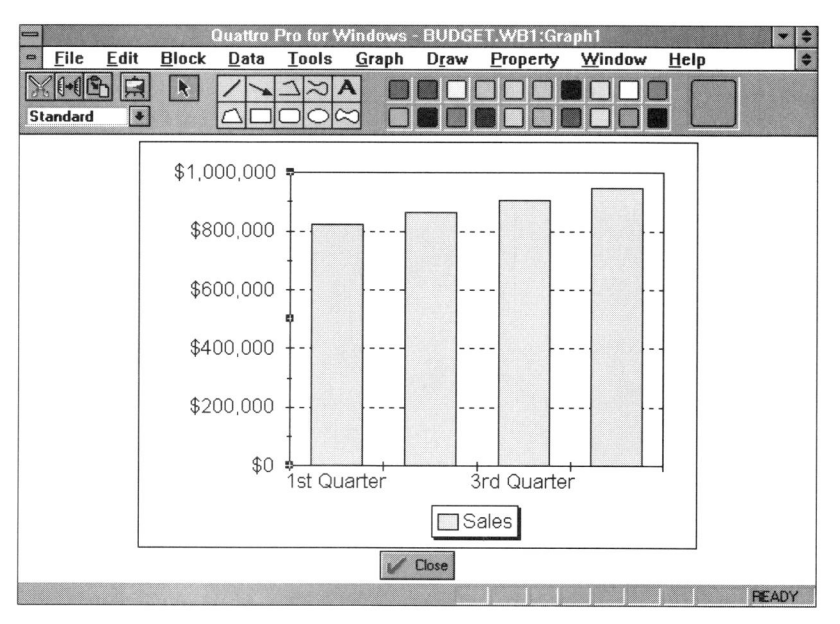

3. Now right-click the legend to display its Object Inspector. For the Legend Position property, click the rightmost button, and then click OK to move the legend from the bottom of the graph to the right side.

4. Click any column in the graph, and then select a color on the Graph SpeedBar. Instantly, the series and its identifier in the legend change color.

5. Click the Close button.

You can use the icons on the graphs page to perform basic operations, like the following:

Graph SpeedBar

In addition to the Cut, Copy, and Paste buttons, the Graph Speedbar has a number of tools to assist you in creating text graphs. You use the various drawing tools to create lines, arrows, text, and different shapes. Selecting the colors on the SpeedBar changes the color of selected objects. You can change the color palette by selecting an option from the drop-down list box under the Cut, Copy, and Paste buttons.

Graphs Page SpeedBar

The Graphs Page SpeedBar, which appears when you click the SpeedTab button, includes buttons that enable you to create custom dialog boxes, SpeedBars, and Slide Shows. Slide Shows are just what they sound like—presentations of graphs in slide-show fashion. You group together graphs and customize Slide Shows using the Slide Show Light Table. For example, you can use the Light Table to edit Slide Shows and add movie-like transition effects between slides. These features are all beyond the scope of this book, but we encourage you to explore them on your own once you are more familiar with Quattro Pro for Windows.

1. Back on the Graphs page, right-click the Graph1 icon, rename it *SINGLE SERIES*, and click OK.

2. Choose Delete from the Graph menu, select Graph2, and click OK. Quattro Pro deletes the second graph you created from the graphs page. If you click the SpeedTab button to return to page A, you'll see that the floating graph has been deleted as well.

3. On the Graphs page, click the SINGLE SERIES icon, and click the Copy button.

4. Click the SpeedTab button to return to page A, and then click the Paste button. Quattro Pro inserts a floating copy of SINGLE SERIES on page A. (You may have to scroll around to find it.) You can now use the graph's handles to move or resize it. ← Moving to page A

5. Choose Save from the File menu.

Creating Picture Graphs

Before we discuss printing graphs, we can't resist mentioning a Quattro Pro feature that allows you to use graphics created in programs such as Paintbrush to plot data series in column or bar graphs. You start by creating a two-dimensional column or bar graph in Quattro Pro. Then you create a simple graphic element in a Windows graphics program and copy it. After opening the graph in its own window, you select the

Draw menu

The commands on the Draw menu affect placement, alignment, and grouping of selected graph objects and objects you've drawn in a text graph. Overlapping graph and draw objects are considered to be in a "stack," with one object on top of another. Use commands like Bring To Front to change the order of the object in the stack. Use commands on the Align submenu to align selected objects to the left, right, top, or bottom, or to center them. Use the Group command to group together multiple objects so that formatting commands affect all members of the group. The Ungroup command disbands the group. Use the Import and Export commands to import graphics into a text graph and to export graphs as graphic images.

series you want the graphic to replace and choose Paste. You can also right-click the series, select the Fill Style category in the series Object Inspector, select the Bitmap option, and click Browse to search for the graphic you want to use. Quattro Pro then substitutes the graphic for the data-series marker, distorting the graphic to fill the area formerly occupied by the column or bar. An example of a picture graph is shown here:

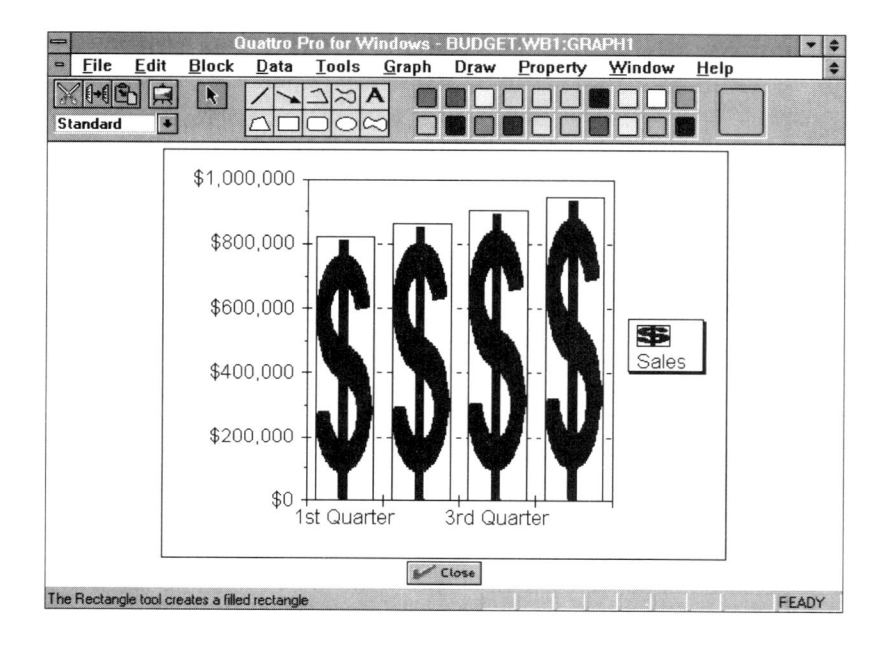

Graphs page icons

The graph icons on the Graphs page reflect the type of graph in the notebook. For example, 3-D graphs appear as three-dimensional graph icons, line graphs appear as line graph icons, and so on. Likewise, slide shows and custom dialog boxes have their own icons on the Graphs page. Custom SpeedBars, however, are saved as separate Quattro Pro documents. To give an icon a more descriptive name, right-click the icon, and enter a name in the dialog box that appears.

Printing Graphs

Printing graphs is much like printing notebooks. The main difference concerns where you print the chart from. When you print from the notebook environment, the graph is printed as it appears on the notebook page, along with the notebook data. When you print from the graph environment, the graph is printed as a full page, without the notebook data. You can use Print Preview to preview a chart, and you can create a header and footer. Although some options in the Page Setup dialog box are unavailable for graphs, the basic procedure is the same as the one outlined in Chapter 2, and you should have no difficulty obtaining paper copies of your graphs.

Notebook environment

Graph environment

5
Estimating Project Costs

Creating the Supporting Tables 110
Counting Entries 115
Creating the Estimate Notebook 116
Looking Up Information 118
Completing the Estimate 120
Projecting Profit Margin with Iteration 121

Creating the estimate notebook
Page 116

Right-aligning entries
Page 113

Circular references
Page 121

Adding commas to values
Page 112

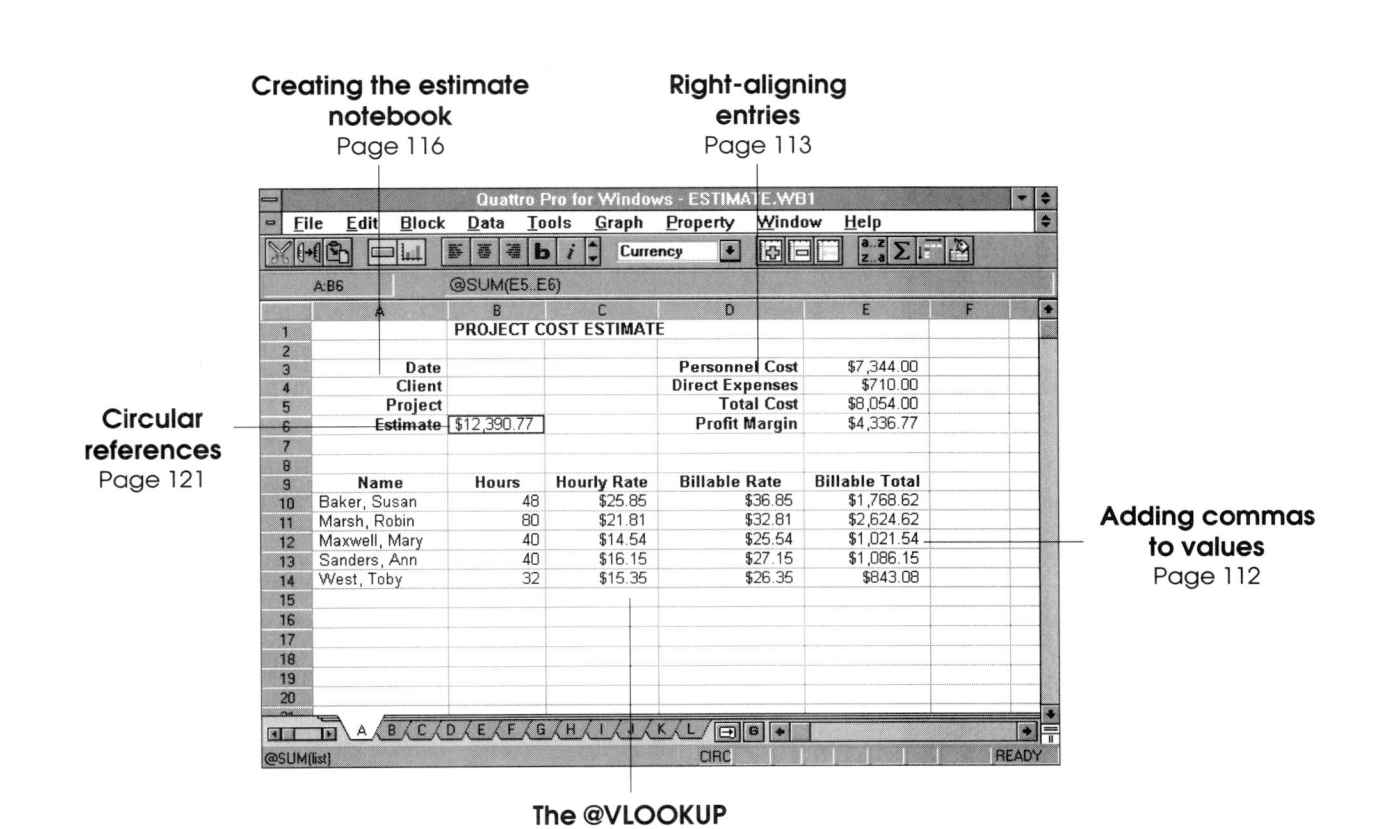

The @VLOOKUP function
Page 118

	A	B	C	D	E	F
1		PROJECT COST ESTIMATE				
2						
3		Date		Personnel Cost	$7,344.00	
4		Client		Direct Expenses	$710.00	
5		Project		Total Cost	$8,054.00	
6		Estimate	$12,390.77	Profit Margin	$4,336.77	
7						
8						
9		Name	Hours	Hourly Rate	Billable Rate	Billable Total
10		Baker, Susan	48	$25.85	$36.85	$1,768.62
11		Marsh, Robin	80	$21.81	$32.81	$2,624.62
12		Maxwell, Mary	40	$14.54	$25.54	$1,021.54
13		Sanders, Ann	40	$16.15	$27.15	$1,086.15
14		West, Toby	32	$15.35	$26.35	$843.08

Cell A:B6 = @SUM(E5..E6)

In this chapter, we tackle a more ambitious set of notebooks. First we create tables of employee information and overhead costs. Then we create a notebook that estimates project costs by "looking up" hourly rates in one of the tables. Finally, we cover a technique called *iteration*, which enables Quattro Pro to resolve circular calculations.

In our example, we create only employee-information and overhead tables because the primary cost involved in the sample cost estimate is for people's time. However, you can easily adapt the cost estimate notebook to incorporate a marketing-expenses or materials-information table. For example, if you manage a construction business that specializes in bathroom and kitchen remodeling, you can create a table with up-to-date prices for fixtures, plumbing supplies, cabinets, tile, and so on, in addition to the employee-information and overhead tables. Even if you are a one-person operation with no employees, you can still adapt the notebook to make sure that you include overhead and marketing costs in your project cost estimates.

This chapter differs from previous chapters in that we don't bog down the instructions with information you already know. For example, we might show you a notebook and ask you to create it, without always telling you step by step what to enter, how to apply formats and styles, and how to adjust column widths. We leave it up to you to create the notebook using the illustration as a guide. Similarly, we might tell you to create a formula, assuming that you know how to enter an @function in a cell and how to click cells to use their addresses as arguments.

In previous chapters, we organized information on multiple notebook pages within a single notebook file. In this chapter, we'll work with three different notebook files, and we'll show you how to create links between them.

Creating the Supporting Tables

The logical way to begin this example is to enter the data needed for the two supporting tables. There's nothing complicated about these tables; we've stripped them down so that

Chapter 5 Estimating Project Costs

you don't have to type any extraneous information. The few calculations involved have been greatly simplified and do not reflect the gyrations accountants would go through to ensure to-the-penny accuracy. So instead of describing in detail how to create these tables, we'll simply show them to you and, after discussing the few formulas and cell and block names involved, let you create them on your own.

1. In a blank notebook, create this table of employee information, and then save it as EMP.WB1:

Employee-information table

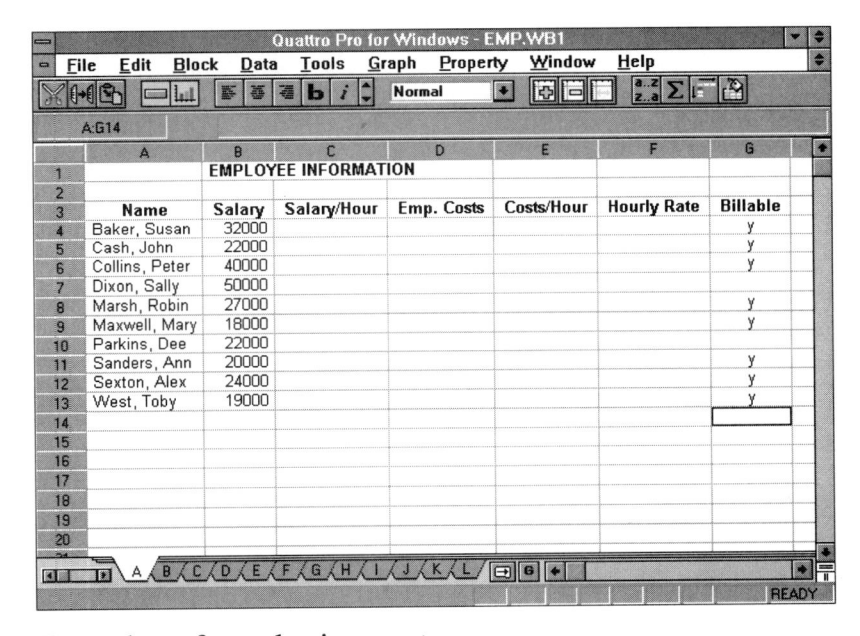

	A	B	C	D	E	F	G
1		EMPLOYEE INFORMATION					
2							
3	Name	Salary	Salary/Hour	Emp. Costs	Costs/Hour	Hourly Rate	Billable
4	Baker, Susan	32000					y
5	Cash, John	22000					y
6	Collins, Peter	40000					y
7	Dixon, Sally	50000					
8	Marsh, Robin	27000					y
9	Maxwell, Mary	18000					y
10	Parkins, Dee	22000					
11	Sanders, Ann	20000					y
12	Sexton, Alex	24000					y
13	West, Toby	19000					y

2. Enter these formulas in row 4:

    C4   +B4/50/30
                Annual salary divided by 50 weeks (allowing 2 weeks for vacation), divided by 30 billable hours per week (allowing 2 hours per day of non-billable time)

    D4   +B4*0.22
                Employer contributions to social security and benefits estimated at 22 percent of annual salary

    E4   +D4/52/30
                Employer contributions to social security and benefits divided by 52 weeks divided by 30 hours per week

    F4   +C4+E4
                Salary per hour plus benefits per hour

Adding commas to values

3. Use the block Object Inspector to set the Numeric Format property for the entries in C4 and E4 to Fixed with 2 decimal places. Then set the same property for the entry in F4 to Fixed with 0 decimal places.

4. Apply the Comma0 style to the entries in B4..B13 and D4.

5. Next, copy the block C4..F4, select C5..F13, and click the Paste button. Here's the result:

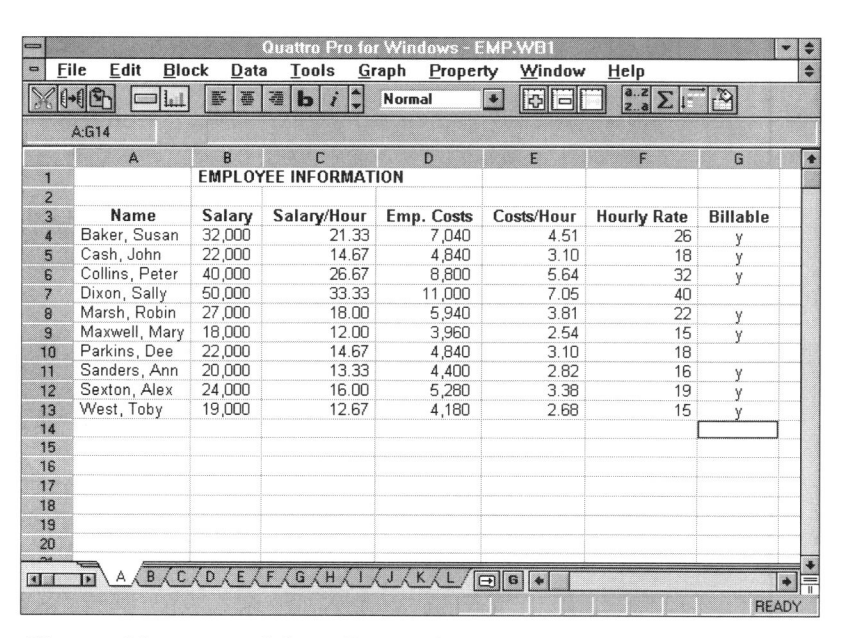

	A	B	C	D	E	F	G
1		EMPLOYEE INFORMATION					
2							
3	Name	Salary	Salary/Hour	Emp. Costs	Costs/Hour	Hourly Rate	Billable
4	Baker, Susan	32,000	21.33	7,040	4.51	26	y
5	Cash, John	22,000	14.67	4,840	3.10	18	y
6	Collins, Peter	40,000	26.67	8,800	5.64	32	y
7	Dixon, Sally	50,000	33.33	11,000	7.05	40	
8	Marsh, Robin	27,000	18.00	5,940	3.81	22	y
9	Maxwell, Mary	18,000	12.00	3,960	2.54	15	y
10	Parkins, Dee	22,000	14.67	4,840	3.10	18	
11	Sanders, Ann	20,000	13.33	4,400	2.82	16	y
12	Sexton, Alex	24,000	16.00	5,280	3.38	19	y
13	West, Toby	19,000	12.67	4,180	2.68	15	y

6. Choose Names and then Create from the Block menu to assign the name BILLABLE to G4..G13 and the name EMP_RATE to A4..F13. (See page 39 for information about how to assign block names.) We'll use these names later to create links to this notebook from other notebooks.

7. Save the notebook.

That's it for the employee-information table. Let's move on to the overhead table.

1. Choose New from the File menu to open a new notebook without closing EMP.WB1. Then create the following overhead table, and save this notebook as OVERHEAD.WB1:

Extending block names

It is sometimes a good idea to include a blank cell or row at the end of the block when you assign a block name. For example, if you need to add employees to the EMP.WB1 notebook, you can select the blank row below the last entry and click the Insert button to extend the block named BILLABLE by one row.

Chapter 5 Estimating Project Costs

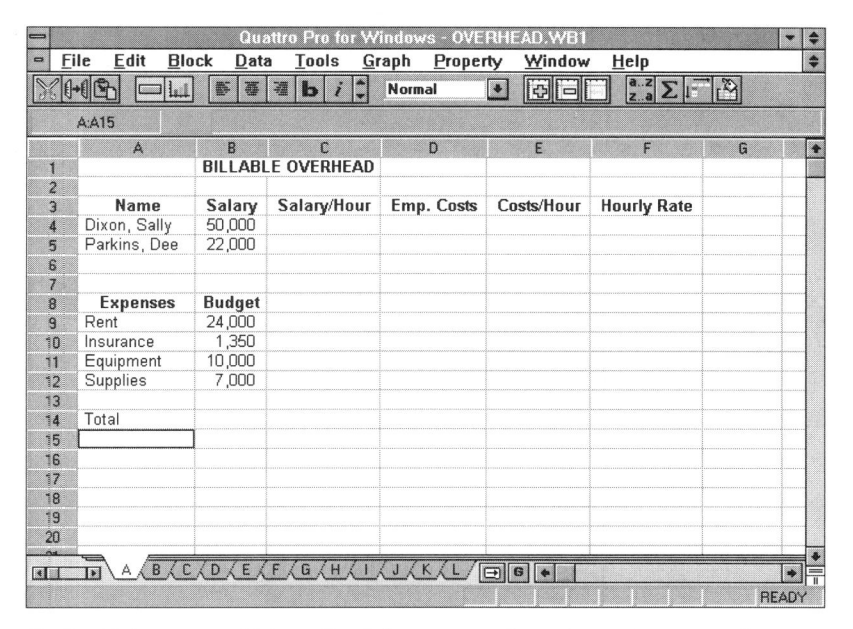

```
                Quattro Pro for Windows - OVERHEAD.WB1
  File  Edit  Block  Data  Tools  Graph  Property  Window  Help

          A          B         C           D          E          F         G
  1              BILLABLE OVERHEAD
  2
  3       Name      Salary   Salary/Hour  Emp. Costs  Costs/Hour  Hourly Rate
  4    Dixon, Sally  50,000
  5    Parkins, Dee  22,000
  6
  7
  8     Expenses    Budget
  9    Rent         24,000
 10    Insurance     1,350
 11    Equipment    10,000
 12    Supplies      7,000
 13
 14    Total
 15
```

2. Sally Dixon and Dee Parkins are administrative employees who do not directly generate income for the company, so we need to include their salaries and benefits in this overhead calculation. You can use the Copy and Paste buttons to copy their entries from the EMP.WB1 notebook, or you can enter the information from scratch. If you choose to use the latter approach, here are the formulas to use in row 4:

C4	+B4/50/30
D4	+B4*0.22
E4	+D4/52/30
F4	+C4+E4

Calculating overhead

3. Set the Numeric Format property for the entries in C4 and E4 to Fixed with 2 decimal places. Then set the same property for the entry in F4 to Fixed with 0 decimal places.

4. Copy the entries in row 4 to row 5.

5. Enter *Expenses/Hour* in cell E14 and *Overhead/Hour* in cell E16, and use the Bold button to make the labels bold. Then make column E wide enough for the Expenses/Hour label, and right-align the text using the Align Right button. The result is shown on the next page.

Right-aligning entries

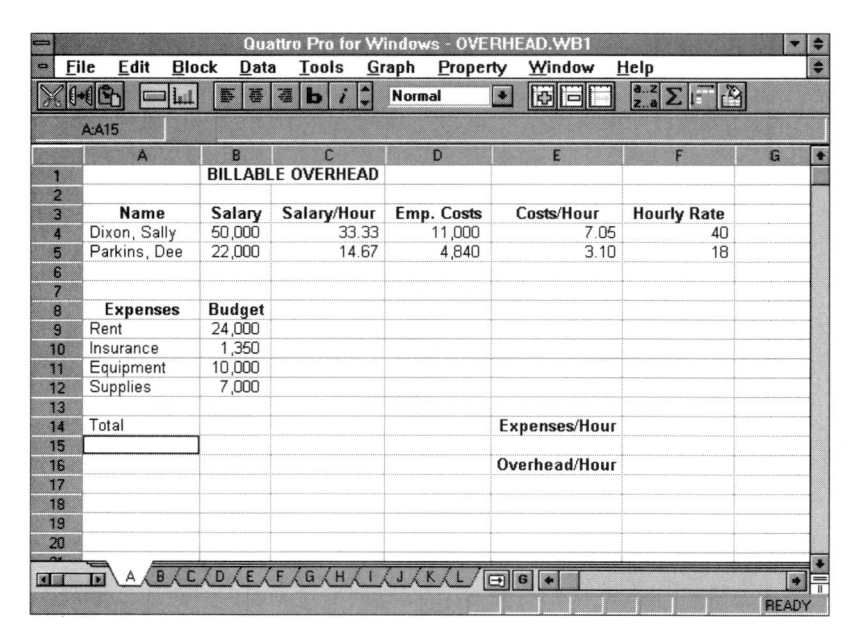

6. Next, enter these formulas in the designated cells:

B14	@SUM(B9..B12)
F14	@ROUND(B14/52/30,0)
	Total expenses divided by 52 weeks divided by 30 hours per week
F16	@SUM(F4..F14)

7. Format B14 with the Comma0 style and F16 as Fixed with 0 decimal places.

We must bill 30 hours each week at the rate in F16 to cover overhead costs. We cannot bill overhead to a client directly, so we must increase the hourly rate of employees with billable hours by a prorated amount to ensure that overhead is included in project estimates. To calculate the prorated overhead amount, we need to divide the total billable rate per hour in cell F16 by the number of employees who generate income. We can glance at the employee-information notebook and quickly tally the employees whose hours are billable, but what if the company had many employees? We need to link the employee-information notebook and the overhead notebook so that Quattro Pro can supply the number of employees for us.

Counting Entries

We can tell Quattro Pro to count the number of employees who have a *y* entry in the Billable column of EMP.WB1 by using the @COUNT function, which finds the number of nonblank cells in the block. This function's argument is the block of cells we want Quattro Pro to scan for entries. Here's how to use @COUNT in the formula that calculates the overhead allocation:

The @COUNT function

1. In cell E17 of OVERHEAD.WB1, type *Prorated/Hour*, and click the ✓ button. Then right-align the label and make it bold.

2. We want the prorated amount to be in whole dollars, so we need to nest the prorated calculation in an @ROUND function. In cell F17, type the following:

   @ROUND(F16/@COUNT(

3. To divide the hourly overhead in cell F16 by the number of employees whose hours are billable, you must now insert a reference to the block that you defined as BILLABLE in the EMP.WB1 notebook. Without moving the insertion point, type *[EMP]* to reference EMP.WB1. Then choose EMP.WB1 from the Window menu, and press the F3 function key to display the Block Names dialog box. Quattro Pro displays the block names you have defined on the EMP.WB1 notebook, like this:

Referencing other notebooks

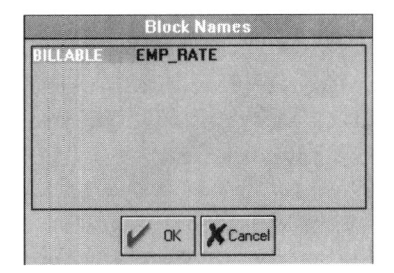

4. Because the name BILLABLE is already highlighted in the list, you can simply click OK. In response, Quattro Pro inserts a reference to the block named BILLABLE, thereby linking the two notebooks. Next, type a *)* to close the @COUNT function. Then type a comma, *0*, and a final *)* to close the @ROUND function.

Flexible formulas

Keep in mind that using names in formulas makes your notebooks much more flexible than using cell references. If the information referenced in a formula moves because of changes you make to a notebook, Quattro Pro adjusts the definition of the name so that it can continue to access the correct information.

5. Check that the following formula is in the input line:

   @ROUND(F16/@COUNT([EMP]BILLABLE),0)

   and then click the ✓ button. Quattro Pro calculates the formula and enters the value 11 in cell F17, as you can see here:

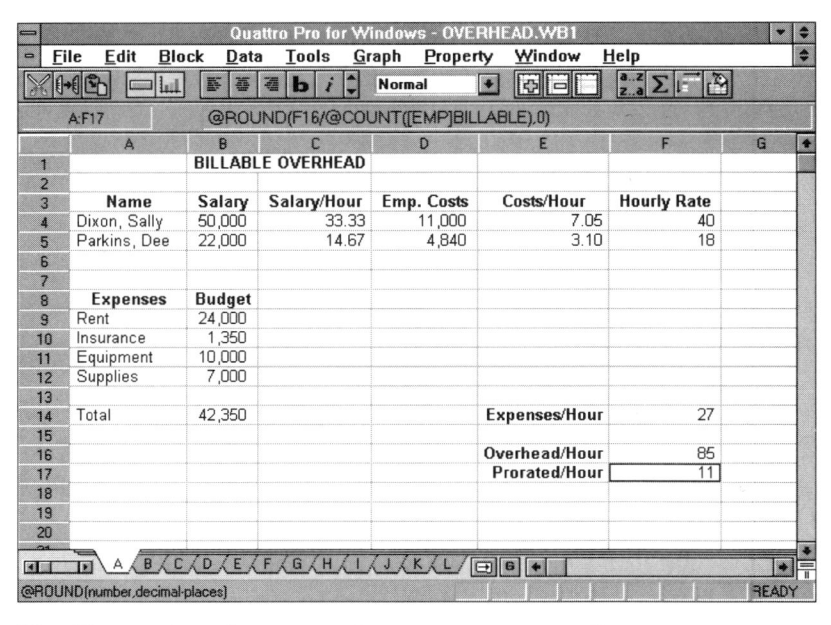

6. Finally, assign the name OVER_RATE to cell F17.

Creating the Estimate Notebook

With the two tables in place, we're ready to create the notebook for estimating project costs. We'll put the basic structure

Smart links

Once you have entered a file reference to establish a link between two notebooks, Quattro Pro will be able to locate the information it needs whether or not the referenced notebook is open.

"Open sesame"

Although Quattro Pro updates external references without opening the referenced notebooks, you can easily open all supporting notebooks by choosing Update Links and then Open Links from the Tools menu. Quattro Pro displays a dialog box listing all notebooks that are referred to by formulas in the active notebook. Simply select the files you want to open, and click the OK button.

of the notebook in place first, and then we'll fill in the formulas necessary for the calculations.

1. Choose New from the File menu to open another notebook. Save this file as ESTIMATE.WB1.

2. Enter the text and formatting shown below. (Use the Speed-Format button or the properties in the block Object Inspector to format the table.) The hours next to the employee names are the number of hours you anticipate each will need to work on this project.

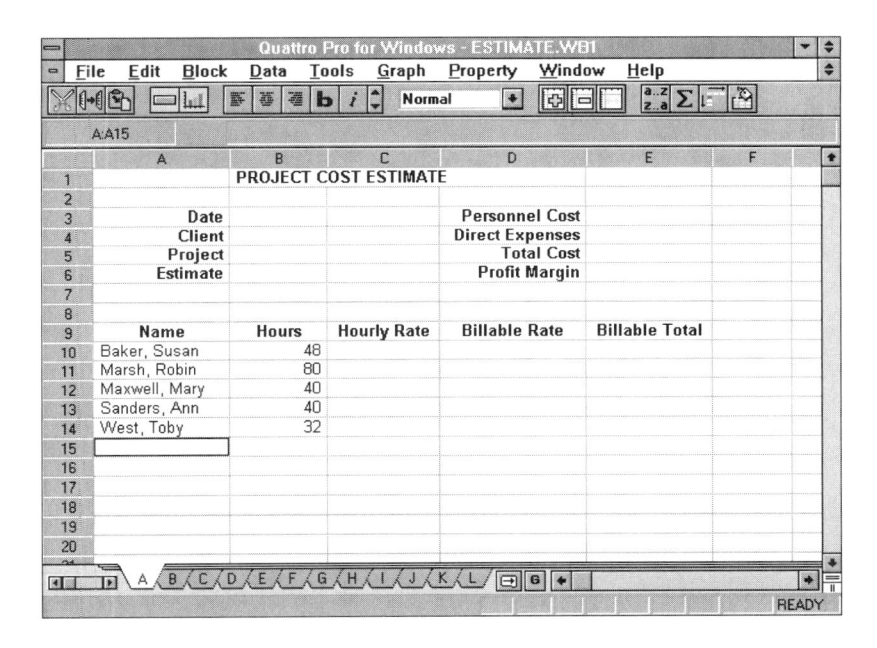

	A	B	C	D	E
1		PROJECT COST ESTIMATE			
2					
3	Date			Personnel Cost	
4	Client			Direct Expenses	
5	Project			Total Cost	
6	Estimate			Profit Margin	
7					
8					
9	Name	Hours	Hourly Rate	Billable Rate	Billable Total
10	Baker, Susan	48			
11	Marsh, Robin	80			
12	Maxwell, Mary	40			
13	Sanders, Ann	40			
14	West, Toby	32			

Saving your workspace

If you always use certain notebooks together, you might find it tiresome to open these files one at a time using the Open command. An easy alternative is to use the Workspace command on the File menu. First, open all the notebooks you'll be working with, and position and resize them as you like. Choose Workspace and then Save from the File menu. Enter a name for the workspace in the File Name edit field, and click OK. The workspace file is simply a list of all the files you had open when you created the workspace, together with their size and position, and even whether the window is hidden or visible. To open all the workspace files, choose Workspace and then Restore from the File menu.

So far, everything has been pretty straightforward and has provided you with nothing more challenging than an opportunity to practice skills you learned in other chapters. Now we'll introduce the Quattro Pro function that will enable you to use data from the employee-information table to complete the cost estimate notebook.

Looking Up Information

Quattro Pro has a variety of @functions you can use in formulas to look up information in notebook tables. Among them are @VLOOKUP (for vertically oriented tables), and @HLOOKUP (for horizontally oriented tables). Here, we'll show you how to use @VLOOKUP.

The @VLOOKUP function

Quattro Pro needs three pieces of information to carry out the @VLOOKUP function: the entry you want it to look up, the block reference of the lookup table, and the column number in the table from which the function should copy a value. (Quattro Pro numbers the first column 0, the second 1, and so on.) To search for a label in the lookup table, you supply these three pieces of information in this way:

@VLOOKUP(*value,block,column*)

Quattro Pro searches down the leftmost column of the block you specify as the second argument for the row that contains the label you supply as the first argument. Then, if it finds the specified label, @VLOOKUP returns the value from the intersection of that row and the column you specify as the third argument. For example, to look up the hourly rate for John Cash in the employee-information table, you can enter the following function, say in cell A19 of EMP.WB1:

@VLOOKUP("Cash, John",A4..G13,5)

Quattro Pro scans the leftmost column—column A—of the table in A4..G13 for the text entry *Cash, John*. When it finds the entry it's looking for in cell A5, it looks across the same row to column F—column 5 (remember, column A is column 0)—and copies the value from cell F5 to cell A19.

Let's see how to put the @VLOOKUP function to work in the project cost estimate notebook:

Chapter 5 Estimating Project Costs

1. Select C10 of ESTIMATE.WB1. Format the cell with the Currency style, and then start entering this formula:

   @VLOOKUP(A10,[EMP.WB1]$EMP_RATE

   The dollar sign before the block name makes the reference absolute. This step is necessary because you are going to copy the formula into other cells in column C and you want the reference to the lookup table to remain unchanged in each copy.

   ◄── **Making references absolute**

2. Enter *,5)* to complete the formula, and click the ✓ button. Quattro Pro checks the value in cell A10 of ESTIMATE.WB1 (*Baker, Susan*), finds that value in the table called EMP_RATE in EMP.WB1, and enters the corresponding hourly rate from column F of the table, as shown here:

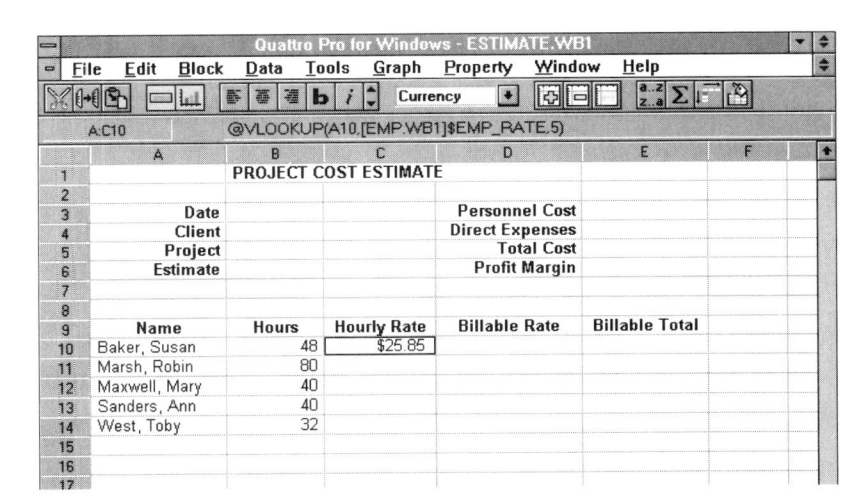

Calculation options

With the default Background Calculation option turned on, Quattro Pro calculates formulas when you enter them and recalculates any existing formulas in open notebooks that are affected by the new entry. If you turn on the Automatic Calculation option, you have to wait until Quattro Pro finishes calculating to continue working.

Manual calculation

You can select the Manual option in the Recalc Settings property of the notebook Object Inspector to tell Quattro Pro to calculate all formulas in a notebook only when you press the F9 function key. You might want to activate this option for large notebooks, where recalculating all the formulas can take some time. The CALC indicator appears in the status line when a formula needs to be recalculated.

Order of recalculation

Quattro Pro can recalculate your notebooks in three ways. Selecting Natural in the Recalc Settings property of the notebook Object Inspector tells Quattro Pro to calculate the current formula after recalculating the formulas it depends on. Selecting Column-wise tells Quattro Pro to move column by column, recalculating formulas as it goes. And selecting Row-wise tells Quattro Pro to move row by row.

3. Now all you have to do is copy C10 in ESTIMATE.WB1, select C11..C14, and click the Paste button to enter equivalent formulas that look up the hourly rates for the other people who will be involved in the project. When you complete this copy operation, examine the newly entered formulas, and notice that the absolute reference to the lookup table (EMP_RATE) has been copied unchanged to each one.

Completing the Estimate

Well, the hard part is over. A few simple calculations, and you'll be ready to prepare an estimate for your client.

1. In ESTIMATE.WB1, enter the following formulas in the indicated cells, and then apply the Currency style to the results:

   D10   +C10+[OVERHEAD]$OVER_RATE
   Hourly rate plus prorated overhead

   E10   +B10*D10

   Notice that the formula in cell D10 contains an absolute reference to the cell named OVER_RATE in the OVERHEAD notebook.

2. Use the Copy and Paste buttons to copy the formulas to cells D11..E14.

Now you can calculate total costs in the summary area at the top of the notebook:

1. Make these entries in the indicated cells, and format them with the Currency style:

   E3   @SUM(E10..E14)

   E4   710
   An estimate of charges for long-distance phone calls, delivery services, and other expenses attributable directly to the project

   E5   +E3+E4

As you can see, this notebook is almost complete:

Chapter 5 Estimating Project Costs

```
Quattro Pro for Windows - ESTIMATE.WB1
File  Edit  Block  Data  Tools  Graph  Property  Window  Help

A:E5            +E3+E4

         A          B         C            D              E         F
 1                      PROJECT COST ESTIMATE
 2
 3           Date                       Personnel Cost   $7,344.00
 4           Client                     Direct Expenses    $710.00
 5           Project                    Total Cost       $8,054.00
 6           Estimate                   Profit Margin
 7
 8
 9           Name     Hours   Hourly Rate  Billable Rate  Billable Total
10   Baker, Susan     48      $25.85       $36.85         $1,768.62
11   Marsh, Robin     80      $21.81       $32.81         $2,624.62
12   Maxwell, Mary    40      $14.54       $25.54         $1,021.54
13   Sanders, Ann     40      $16.15       $27.15         $1,086.15
14   West, Toby       32      $15.35       $26.35           $843.08
15
...
                                                                READY
```

Projecting Profit Margin with Iteration

Probably the most difficult part of estimating a project is figuring out the profit margin. We now have a good idea what this project is going to cost. But suppose we need a margin of roughly 35 percent of the estimate total to be sure we make a profit. How do we calculate the actual profit margin when we don't yet know the estimate total, and how do we calculate the estimate total when we don't know the profit margin? We could go in circles forever.

Fortunately, we can have Quattro Pro go in circles for us. Using the iteration technique, we can force Quattro Pro to calculate the margin formula over and over until it can give us an answer. Follow these steps:

Circular references

1. Select E6 in the ESTIMATE.WB1 notebook, format the cell with the Currency style, and enter this formula:

   0.35*B6

2. Now select B6, format it with the Currency style, and enter this formula:

   @SUM(E5..E6)

3. When you enter the second formula, Quattro Pro enters an estimate value in E6, and the CIRC indicator appears in the status line. Quattro Pro displays this indicator because the formula in B6 contains a reference to cell E6, and the formula in E6 contains a reference to B6.

4. To get more information about a circular reference, choose Active Notebook from the Property menu to open the notebook Object Inspector. Quattro Pro identifies the location of the circular reference in the Recalc Settings property:

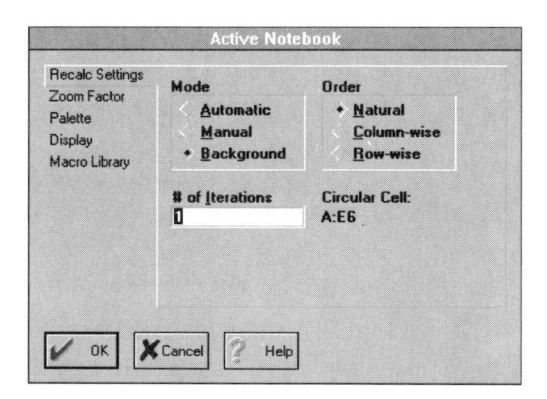

By default, Quattro Pro calculates a formula once, which is what most formulas require. You now need to instruct Quattro Pro to calculate the formulas in B6 and E6 many times—in an iterative process—until a reasonable estimate is found for the profit margin.

Opening circular notebooks

Occasionally when you open a notebook that has a circular reference that uses values in other notebooks, formulas relying on the circular reference are replaced by NA error values. To see the results of the iterative calculation process, select one of the cells involved in the circular reference, activate the input line, and press Enter. Quattro Pro then recalculates the formulas and displays the result. If you want to retain the values without going through this process each time you reopen the notebook, copy the results, choose Paste Special from the Edit menu, select Values Only, and click OK to paste just the values somewhere else.

Chapter 5 Estimating Project Costs

5. Set the number of iterations to 50, and click OK.

Specifying iterations

6. When you return to the notebook, press F9, the recalculation function key. Quattro Pro quickly recalculates the formulas, finally coming up with these results:

PROJECT COST ESTIMATE

	B	C	D	E
Date			Personnel Cost	$7,344.00
Client			Direct Expenses	$710.00
Project			Total Cost	$8,054.00
Estimate	$12,390.77		Profit Margin	$4,336.77

Name	Hours	Hourly Rate	Billable Rate	Billable Total
Baker, Susan	48	$25.85	$36.85	$1,768.62
Marsh, Robin	80	$21.81	$32.81	$2,624.62
Maxwell, Mary	40	$14.54	$25.54	$1,021.54
Sanders, Ann	40	$16.15	$27.15	$1,086.15
West, Toby	32	$15.35	$26.35	$843.08

By using iteration, you have told Quattro Pro to keep recalculating the formula, going in circles for 50 iterations. The result might not be exact, but inaccuracies of less than a penny are not likely to cause concern.

You now have a completed project estimate that takes into account your company's overhead costs as well as the direct costs associated with the project. As we said at the beginning of the chapter, you can adapt this set of notebooks in many ways to help you quickly assemble bids. You can also use the notebooks to compare the cost of doing projects in-house with estimates that you receive from vendors. And once you have set up a lookup table such as the employee-information table, you can link it to notebooks that perform a variety of other personnel-related calculations.

Quattro Pro Macros

Setting Up an Invoice 126
Creating Macros 128
Recording Macros 129
Defining Macros from Scratch 132
Assigning Macros to Buttons 134
Logging Invoice Data with a Macro 136
Setting Up the Invoice Log 136
Creating the Log Macro 137
Running the Macro 138
If the Macro Doesn't Work 138

The Address macro
Page 133

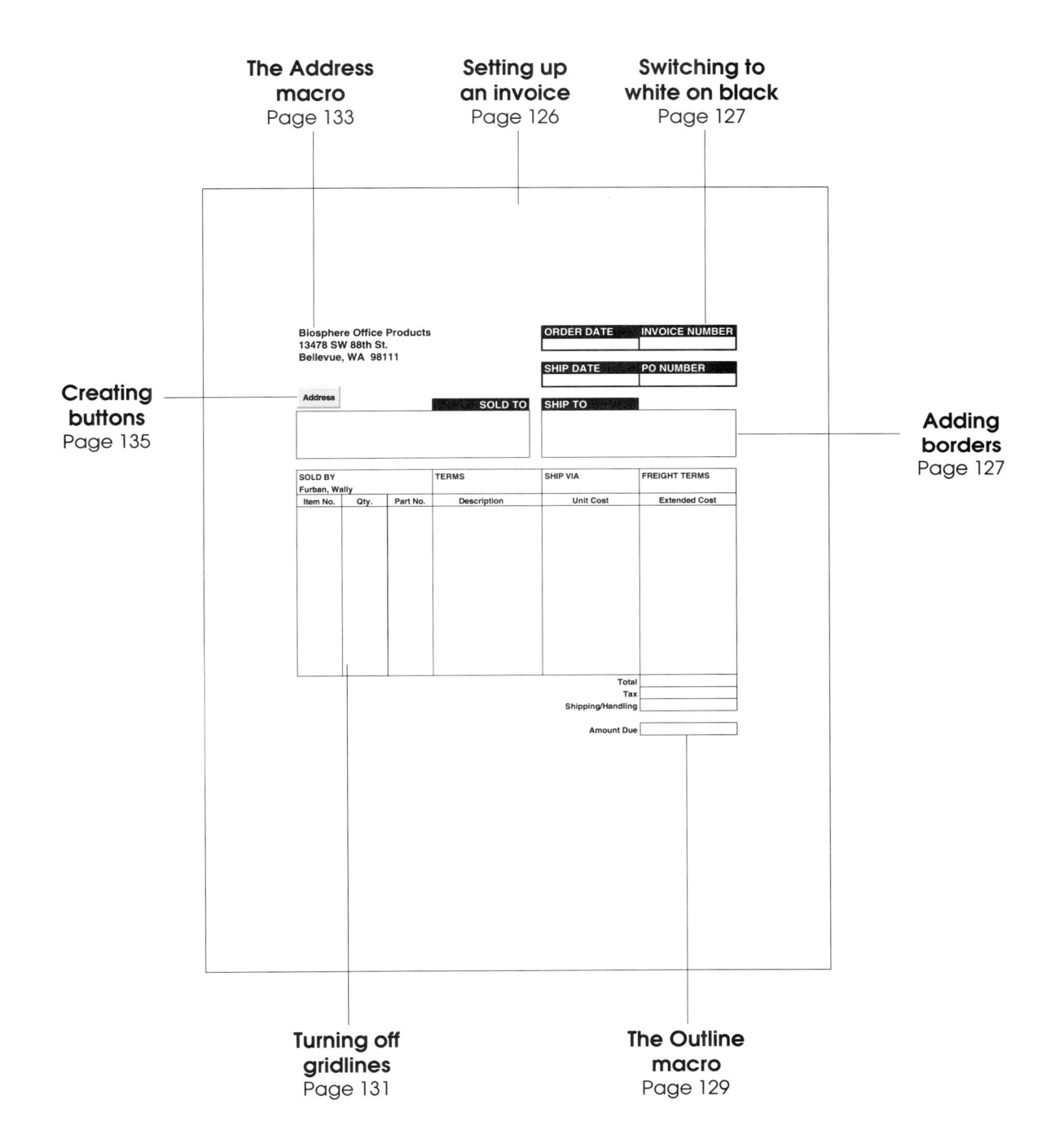

Setting up an invoice
Page 126

Switching to white on black
Page 127

Creating buttons
Page 135

Adding borders
Page 127

Turning off gridlines
Page 131

The Outline macro
Page 129

Biosphere Office Products
13478 SW 88th St.
Bellevue, WA 98111

ORDER DATE | INVOICE NUMBER

SHIP DATE | PO NUMBER

Address

SOLD TO | SHIP TO

SOLD BY
Furban, Wally

| Item No. | Qty. | Part No. | Description | Unit Cost | Extended Cost |

TERMS | SHIP VIA | FREIGHT TERMS

Total
Tax
Shipping/Handling
Amount Due

In this final chapter, we demonstrate the Quattro Pro macro feature, which can greatly increase your efficiency by automating some of the routine tasks associated with setting up notebooks. After you master the basics, even those of you who get sweaty palms at the thought of having to deal with something as "techie" as a macro language will begin thinking of ways to put macros to use.

The example for this chapter is an invoice. In Chapter 3, we told you that we would show you a way to avoid having to manually input data into databases like invoice logs. The key to streamlining the data-input process is to generate forms, such as invoices, in Quattro Pro and then use a macro to make Quattro Pro do the work of transferring the data from the invoices to the invoice log.

Setting Up an Invoice

The invoice we are going to create in this chapter is shown on the previous page. Take a quick look to get oriented, and then let's get going.

1. Open a new notebook, and save it as INVOICE.WB1.

2. Make the following entries in the indicated cells:

F1	ORDER DATE
G1	INVOICE NUMBER
F4	SHIP DATE
G4	PO NUMBER
D7	SOLD TO
F7	SHIP TO
A13	SOLD BY
D13	TERMS
F13	SHIP VIA
G13	FREIGHT TERMS
A15	Item No.
B15	Qty.
C15	Part No.
D15	Description
F15	Unit Cost
G15	Extended Cost
F30	Total
F31	Tax
F32	Shipping/Handling
F34	Amount Due

Now we'll do some formatting. We won't spell out every last detail because by now you should have a good idea of how to track down commands and handle their dialog boxes.

1. Use the Column Width property of the block Object Inspector to adjust the column widths as follows:

   A, B, C   8
   D, F, G   19
   E   1

2. Use the Bold button on the SpeedBar to make all the cell entries bold.

3. Hold down Ctrl, and select F1, G1, F4, G4, D7, and F7. Select the Shading property of the block Object Inspector, and click Black in the Color 1 box and Solid Black in the Blend box to make the cells black. Then use the Text Color property to change the text color to white so that it stands out against the black background. Click OK to apply the formatting.

   Switching to white on black

4. Hold down Ctrl, and select F1..F2, G1..G2, F4..F5, and G4..G5. Then use the Line Drawing property of the block Object Inspector to outline the cells with a thick border. (Select the thick Line Type and then the Outline option.)

   Adding borders

5. Use the alignment buttons on the SpeedBar to center the entries in row 15 and right-align the entries in D7 and F30..F34.

6. Select the following blocks, and use the Font property of the block Object Inspector to reduce the size of the text to 8 points:

   F2..G2   A8..D11   A13..G34
   F5..G5   F8..G11

7. Because you will be entering dates in two of the boxes at the top of the screen, let's format those cells now. Select F2 and F5. Then in the Number Format property of the block Object Inspector, select the Short Date Intl. format, and click OK.

8. Format the cells in the Unit Cost and Extended Cost columns (F16..G34) as dollars and cents by selecting them and then selecting Currency from the Style list.

9. Save the notebook.

   With that out of the way, let's take a look at macros.

Template notebooks

If you repeatedly use the same basic notebook structure, you might want to save that notebook as a template. Then you can open the template, make any custom entries you need, and save the notebook with a new name to preserve the template for future use. For example, you might save INVOICE.WB1 as a template and then save filled-in invoices with their invoice numbers as their filenames.

Creating Macros

A macro is a set of instructions, recorded in a column of a notebook. When you run a macro, Quattro Pro moves sequentially down the column of instructions, doing whatever it is told to do. The Quattro Pro macro language includes special instructions enclosed in curly braces ({ and }) that emulate keyboard strokes, mouse actions, and menu commands. For example, {Edit Copy} chooses the Copy command from the Edit menu, {SelectBlock A:F1} selects cell F1 on page A of the current notebook, and {PutCell John} enters the text "John" in a cell. You'll see examples of all these instructions in the macros we create in this chapter.

A macro contained in a notebook is available for use whenever that notebook is open, and a macro stored in an open macro library (a special type of notebook) can be used to carry out that task in any open notebook. When you create a macro, you normally assign it a special block name consisting of the backslash character and a letter of the alphabet—for example, \B. When you want to run the macro, you simply press Ctrl-B. Quattro Pro then finds the macro named \B and performs its instructions.

The macro recorder

To make it easy for new users to create macros right away, Quattro Pro has a macro recorder that you can use to record a series of keystrokes, mouse clicks, and commands as a macro. Quattro Pro takes care of translating these actions into the macro language and writing them into a block on the notebook. You assign the macro a unique name and shortcut key to distinguish it from other macros in the same notebook. You can then "play back" the macro in one of two ways: You can press Ctrl and the shortcut key; or you can choose Macro and then Execute from the Tools menu, select the macro name, and click OK. You can also link the macro to a "button" on the notebook that you have created using the SpeedButton tool on the SpeedBar; clicking the button then runs the macro.

Our discussion of macros will be necessarily brief and is not intended to make you an instant Quattro Pro macro expert. The idea is to get you thinking about whether tasks you perform routinely could be more efficiently carried out with macros, and to give you enough information to explore the topic further on your own. We start by showing you how to record a macro. Next, we take a look at the process by which you create macros from scratch. Then we assign a macro to a button. Finally, we examine a macro that transfers information from a completed invoice to an invoice log.

Recording Macros

To resemble the invoice at the beginning of the chapter, the invoice now on your screen needs borders around several blocks. Earlier, you created borders manually by selecting the Line Drawing property in the block Object Inspector, selecting a line type, selecting Outline, and then clicking OK. This set of steps is an ideal candidate for a simple recorded macro, so let's get to work.

1. Select A8..D11, the first block you want to outline.

2. Turn on the macro recorder by choosing Macro and then Record from the Tools menu to display this dialog box:

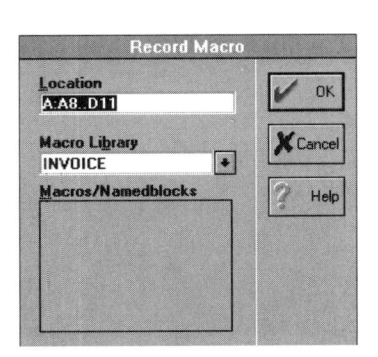

The Outline macro

3. It's a good idea to start macros on their own page because the recorder overwrites anything in the column below the starting cell as it progresses. So replace the reference in the Location field with B:A1 to establish page B as your macro page.

4. Click OK. Quattro Pro displays REC in the status line.

5. Right-click the selected range, and select the Line Drawing property. Select the thinnest line type, select Outline, and then click OK.

6. Choose Macro and then Stop Record from the Tools menu to stop recording.

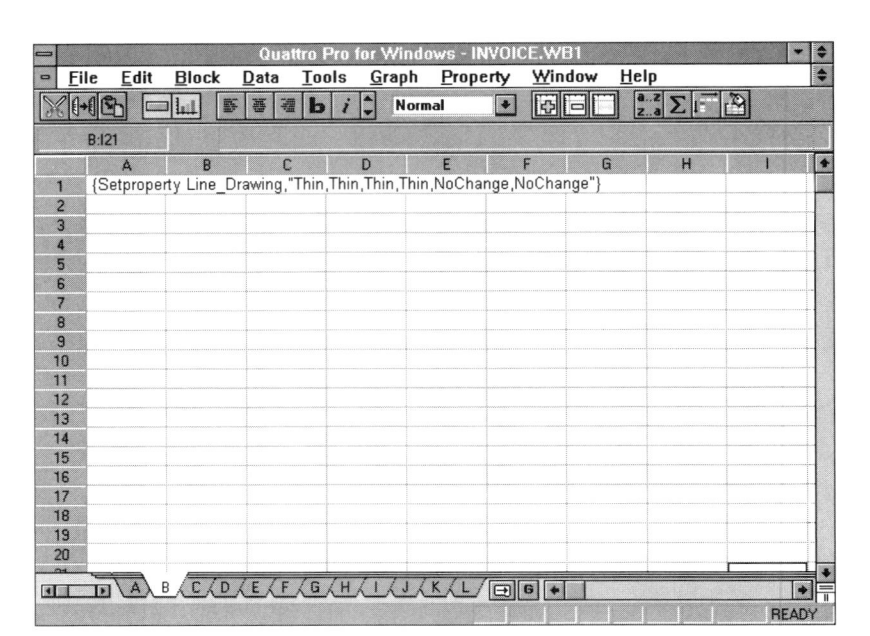

7. Click the page B tab. Quattro Pro interprets your formatting action as this macro command:

```
{Setproperty Line_Drawing,"Thin,Thin,Thin,Thin,NoChange,NoChange"}
```

The four Thin arguments put a thin line on the left, top, right, and bottom borders of a block. The two NoChange arguments refer to the vertical and horizontal cross-lines within a block.

It's a good idea to give your macros descriptive labels on the macro page. For this macro, we'll enter the label *Outline (\o)* to remind us of the macro's function. The \o specifies both the official name and the keystoke you use to invoke the macro (Ctrl-o).

Smart recorder

If you cancel an action or click the Cancel button in a dialog box while Quattro Pro is recording a macro, the action is not recorded. If you Undo an action, Quattro Pro records both the action and the Undo command.

Ending macros

Always leave a blank cell, or use a {Quit} or {Return} command at the end of a macro to complete it. If there is no blank cell or {Quit} or {Return} command and another macro follows, then both macros are executed, one after the other.

Macro comments

In addition to adding a descriptive label to a macro, you can add comments. Enter the descriptive text for each line of the macro in the column to the right of the macro commands. Comments are particularly useful in long, complex macros.

Chapter 6 Quattro Pro Macros 131

1. Insert a column before column A, format the new column A as bold, and enter *Outline (\o)* in cell A1. Widen the column to display the whole label.

2. Select B:B1, and choose Names and then Create from the Block menu. Enter the name \o, and click OK.

Now let's use this macro to format the next block:

1. Return to page A, and select A:F8..A:G11.

2. Choose Macro and then Execute from the Tools menu to display this dialog box:

The Execute command

3. Select \O (Quattro Pro displays names in capital letters, no matter how you enter them), and click OK. Quattro Pro places a border around the block.

Now let's use the shortcut key combination to outline some additional blocks:

1. Select the following cells and blocks, pressing Ctrl-o after each selection:

The shortcut key combination

A:A13..C14	A:F15	A:F16..A:F29
A:D13..A:E14	A:G15	A:G16..A:G29
A:F13..A:F14	A:A16..A:A29	A:G30
A:G13..A:G14	A:B16..A:B29	A:G31
A:A15	A:C16..A:C29	A:G32
A:C15	A:D16..A:E29	A:G34

2. To make the borders stand out, turn off the notebook's gridlines by right-clicking the page tab to display the page Object Inspector. Then select the Grid Lines property, deselect Horizontal and Vertical, and click OK. The result is shown on the next page.

Turning off gridlines

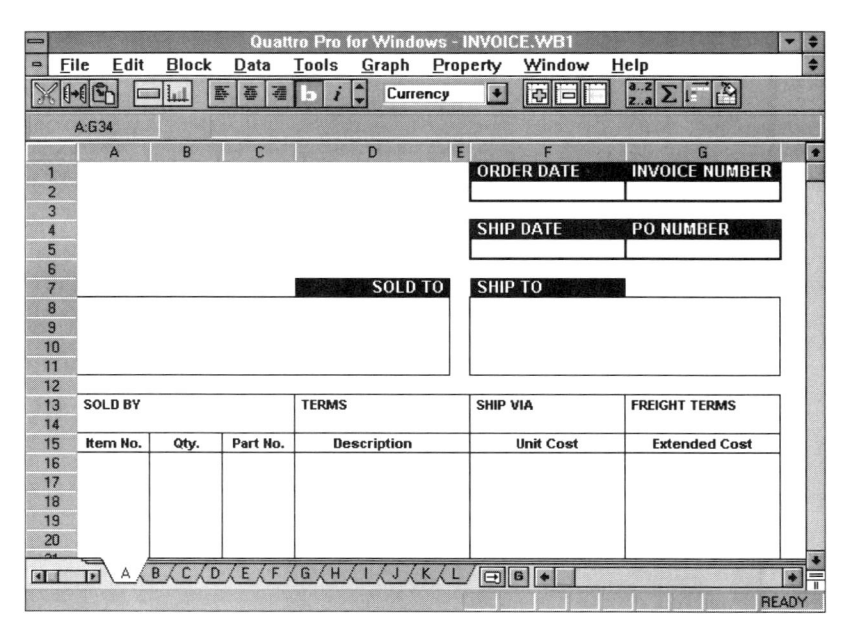

3. Now would be a good time to save the notebook again, to preserve the work you have done so far.

Defining Macros from Scratch

You've probably noticed the blank hole in the top-left corner of the invoice. Let's create a simple macro that will insert a company name and address in this area. In the process, we'll take a look at the macro page and learn something more about the Quattro Pro macro language. First, follow these steps to name the notebook pages we are working with:

Stopping macros

You can stop a macro's progress at any point by pressing Ctrl-Break. Quattro Pro displays a dialog box telling you at what point it stopped the macro. Click OK to close the dialog box and return to the notebook with the rest of the macro instructions unexecuted.

Macro libraries

To save a library of general-purpose macros, you might want to create a separate notebook file. Right-click the notebook title bar (or choose Active Notebook from the Property menu) to display the notebook Object Inspector, select the Macro Library property, select Yes, and click OK. Save the notebook with a name such as MACLIB.WB1, and open the notebook whenever you want to access the macros it contains. To have the macro library open automatically when Quattro Pro starts, open the application Object Inspector, select the Startup property, enter the name of the macro library in the Autoload File field, and click OK.

1. Right-click the page B tab to activate it and open its Object Inspector. Name the page *Macro*.

2. Right-click the page A tab, and name the page *Invoice*.

A thorough examination of Quattro Pro's macro commands is beyond the scope of this book. Suffice it to say that a Quattro Pro macro command probably exists for every common notebook task—and for many uncommon ones, too! You can consult the *Building Spreadsheet Applications* manual for a complete listing of all the macro commands and their arguments. In the meantime, let's combine a few functions to create another macro.

1. In cell A3 of the Macro page, type *Address (\a)*, the new macro's label. ← **The Address macro**

2. To enter the company name and address, type the following macro commands in the indicated cells, exactly as you see them here:

	A	B	C
3	Address (\a)	{SelectBlock A:A1}	Selects A1 of page A of the notebook
4		{PutCell Biosphere Office Products}	Enters the first line of the address in A1
5		{SelectBlock A:A2}	Selects A2
6		{PutCell '13478 SW 88th St.}	Enters the second line of the address
7		{SelectBlock A:A3}	Selects A3
8		{PutCell "Bellevue, WA 98111"}	Enters the third line of the address
9		{SelectBlock A:A1..A3}	Selects A1..A3
10		{SetProperty Font.Bold,Yes}	Makes A1..A3 bold
11		{Return}	End of the macro

You can substitute your own company's name and address if you want. You don't have to type the comments in column C, which explain each function.

3. Select B3, and choose Names and then Create from the Block menu. Enter the name \a for the macro, and click OK.

Now let's test the new macro. Simply follow the steps on the next page.

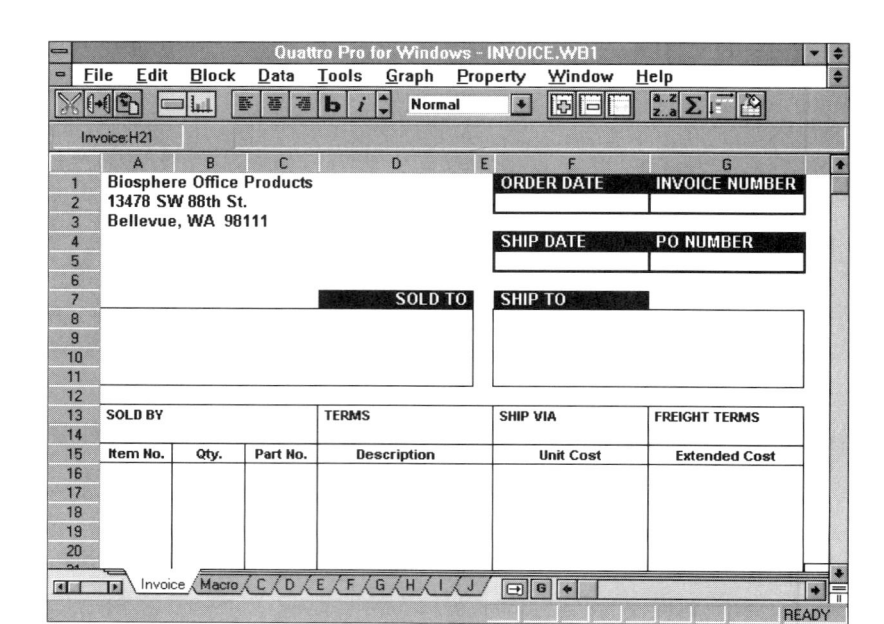

1. From the Macro page, press Ctrl-a to run the macro. Here's the result:

Congratulations. You've just written your first macro.

Assigning Macros to Buttons

As we mentioned earlier, you can assign a macro to a button on the notebook and then run the macro simply by clicking the button. You create the button using the SpeedButton tool on the SpeedBar. Buttons are useful because they provide instant access to macros and because they serve as a graphic reminder of the macros' availability.

Startup macros

You can have Quattro Pro run a macro as soon as you open the notebook that contains it. By default, Quattro Pro automatically runs any macro that has the name \0—the number zero. (You can change the default startup macro name using the Startup property of the application Object Inspector.) Startup macros are handy. For example, you can use a startup macro to hide a macro library so that no one can accidentally alter your macros. Just add a macro consisting of the {WindowHide} instruction to the macro library notebook, and name the macro \0. The next time you open the macro library, Quattro Pro will automatically hide the macro library's window. Use the Show command on the Window menu to redisplay it.

To see how buttons work, try this:

1. Clear the address from cells A1..A3 of INVOICE.WB1.

2. Click the SpeedButton tool on the SpeedBar. The pointer changes to a cross hair.

   Creating buttons

3. Drag the cross-hair pointer to draw a marquee that roughly covers cells A6..C7. Quattro Pro creates a button labeled Button1.

4. Right-click the button to display its Object Inspector menu.

5. Choose Label Text. In the dialog box that appears, enter *Address*, and click OK. Quattro Pro changes the label on the button to Address.

6. Right-click the button again, and choose Macro. In the Enter Macro edit field, type *{branch \a}*, and click OK. You could enter in the Macro dialog box the exact macro commands needed to duplicate the Address macro, but a quicker way is to refer to the macro using the {Branch} command. When you click the button, the {Branch} command tells Quattro Pro to search for the macro named \a and execute it.

   The {Branch} command

7. Click elsewhere on the notebook to deselect the button. Then click the button to run the Address macro. Here's the result:

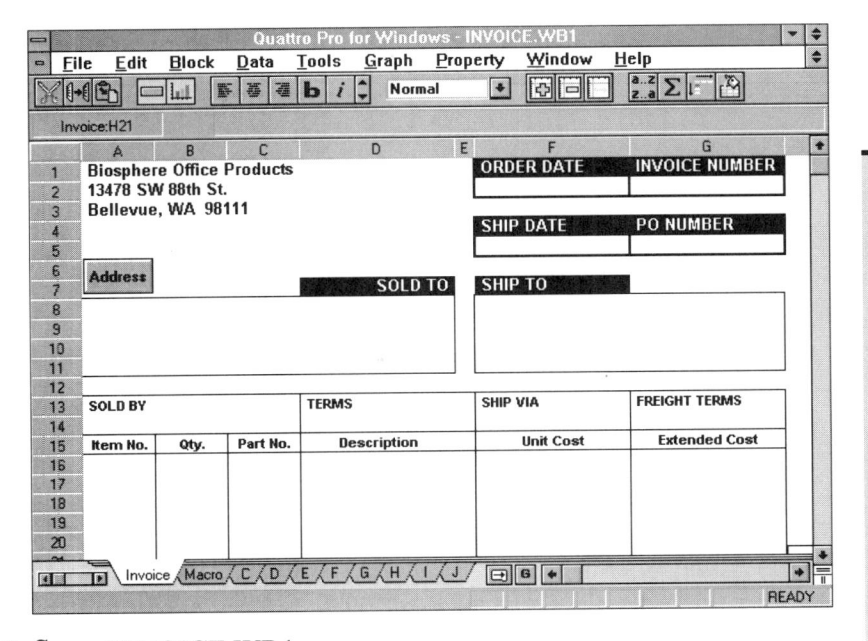

Macro button changes

If you need to assign another macro to the button or you want to change the button name, right-click the button to open its Object Inspector menu. Then choose Macro or Label Text, and make your changes. To move or resize the button, right-click it, and then either drag it to a new position, or drag its handles to resize it.

8. Save INVOICE.WB1.

Logging Invoice Data with a Macro

You now know enough about macros to follow along as we create one that will take the information you enter on the Invoice page and record it in an invoice log. This macro can be adapted for many uses. For example, you could use the techniques you learned while creating the invoice to develop a contacts notebook. You could then adapt the macro to pull information about each new client you work with into a name and address database. Or you might want to create an expense-report notebook and adapt the macro to record expenses in a reimbursement summary.

Adapting the macro

Before we can work on the macro, we need to create the invoice-log notebook page, so let's get started.

Setting Up the Invoice Log

For demonstration purposes, we'll keep this log very simple. Follow these steps:

1. Right-click the page C tab to select it and open the page Object Inspector. Name the page *Log*, and click OK.

2. Make the following entries in the indicated cells:

C1	INVOICE LOG
A3	Date
B3	Invoice Number
C3	Salesperson
D3	Amount of Sale

3. Select A1..D3, and click the Bold button. Then select B1..D3, and click the Fit button.

4. Format column A with the DD-MMM-YY date format, and format column D with the Currency style.

Designating the end of the database

5. We want Quattro Pro to append new invoices to the end of the invoice log, so select A4, choose Names and then Create from the Block menu, and then assign the name END to the selected cell.

6. Return to the Invoice page, and assign the following names to the specified cells:

INVOICE:F2   ORDER_DATE
INVOICE:G2   INV_NUM
INVOICE:A14   SOLD_BY
INVOICE:G34   AMOUNT

7. Save the notebook, leaving it open on your screen.

That's it for the setup work. Now let's move on to create the Log macro.

Creating the Log Macro

The Log macro we are going to create uses a macro command called {Let} to copy data items from the named cells on the Invoice page to the Log page. You will also see examples of the @CELLPOINTER function, which identifies the address of the current cell.

1. Click the Macro page tab to display that page. Enter this macro in the block B:B13..B:B23, and enter the label *Log(\l)* in A13 (again, you don't have to type the comments in column B):

The Log macro

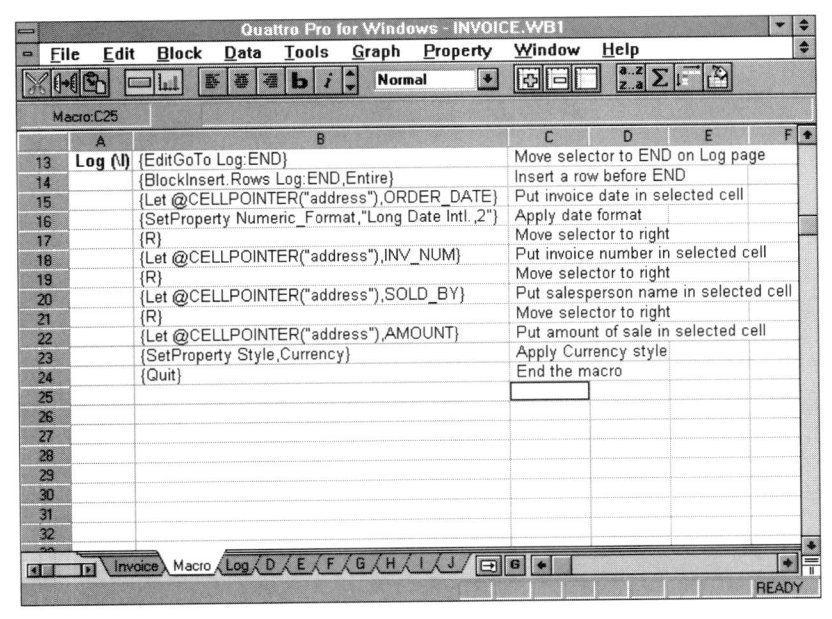

	A	B	C D E F
13	Log (\l)	{EditGoTo Log:END}	Move selector to END on Log page
14		{BlockInsert.Rows Log:END,Entire}	Insert a row before END
15		{Let @CELLPOINTER("address"),ORDER_DATE}	Put invoice date in selected cell
16		{SetProperty Numeric_Format,"Long Date Intl.",2"}	Apply date format
17		{R}	Move selector to right
18		{Let @CELLPOINTER("address"),INV_NUM}	Put invoice number in selected cell
19		{R}	Move selector to right
20		{Let @CELLPOINTER("address"),SOLD_BY}	Put salesperson name in selected cell
21		{R}	Move selector to right
22		{Let @CELLPOINTER("address"),AMOUNT}	Put amount of sale in selected cell
23		{SetProperty Style,Currency}	Apply Currency style
24		{Quit}	End the macro

2. Select B:B13, and choose Names and then Create from the Block menu. Assign the name \l to this cell.

3. Save the notebook again.

Running the Macro

Now for the acid test. We'll make a few entries in the invoice on the Invoice page, and then run the macro. Here goes:

1. Make the following entries in the indicated cells:

   INVOICE:F2   03/09/92 (press Ctrl-Shift-D first)
   INVOICE:G2   '5234AA
   INVOICE:A14   Karnov, Peter
   INVOICE:G34   54687

2. Press Ctrl-l. If you have entered the macro correctly, Quattro Pro transfers the information from the invoice to the invoice log, as shown here:

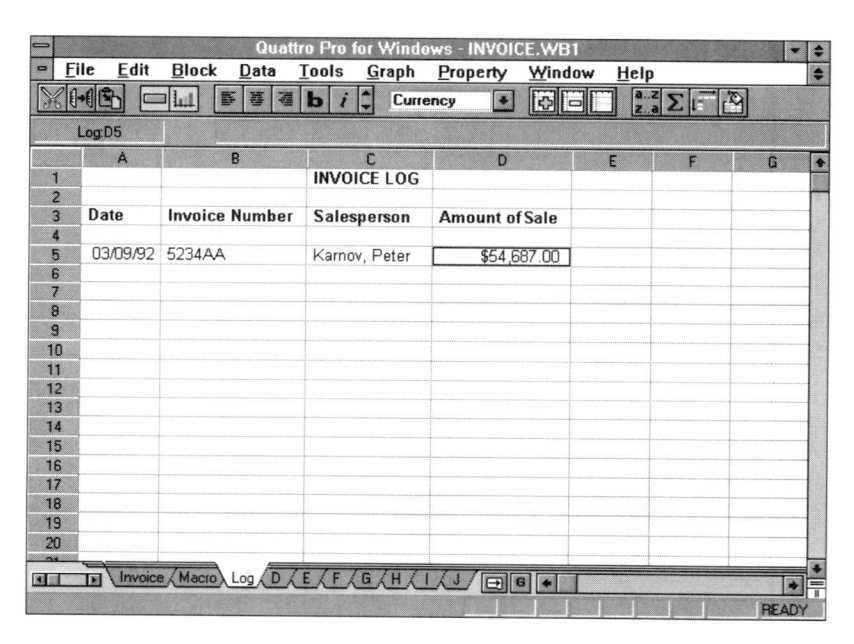

You might want to enter some new values on the Invoice page and press Ctrl-l to run the macro again in order to see how Quattro Pro appends the information from successive invoices to the invoice log.

If the Macro Doesn't Work

Macro error messages

If Quattro Pro encounters a recognizable error in the macro, it stops and displays a message announcing the location of the error. The most likely cause of errors is typos, such as missing or misplaced brackets. On the other hand, Quattro Pro might complete a macro without interruption but produce unexpected results. In the latter case, Quattro Pro offers a way to sleuth out the cause of the problem.

If you choose Macro from the Tools menu and then choose Debugger, Quattro Pro displays DEBUG in the status line. When you start your potentially buggy macro, Quattro Pro displays this Macro Debugger window:

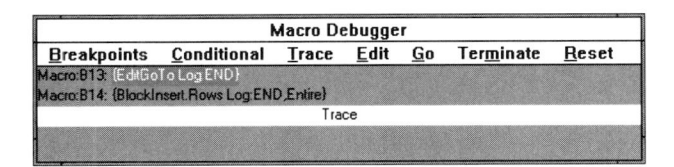

```
                        Macro Debugger
 Breakpoints   Conditional   Trace   Edit   Go   Terminate   Reset
Macro:B13: {EditGoTo Log END}
Macro:B14: {BlockInsert.Rows Log END,Entire}
                             Trace
```

As you can see, the window displays the location of the current macro instruction, along with the instruction itself. To step from one macro instruction to the next, you simply press any key, or click the Trace bar in the window. Quattro Pro highlights the instructions as it carries them out, giving you the opportunity to see the macro in slow motion and spot errors. Click Edit to move to the highlighted instruction in the macro so that you can make changes, click Terminate to end the macro, and click Go to continue the macro at full speed.

Stepping through the macro

Well, that quick overview of macros winds up the book. You are now equipped with the skills you need to create some pretty sophisticated notebooks and should be familiar enough with Quattro Pro to explore on your own.

Index

$ (absolute reference) 57
' (left-align prefix character) 8
* (asterisk) 10
... (ellipsis) 14
3 button 5
@ button 50
^ (center prefix character) 8
{ } (curly braces) 128
" (right-align prefix character) 8

A

absolute references 57, 119, 120
active
   cell 4–5, 12–13
      moving 5, 20
   notebook 17–18
Active Notebook command 122, 132
adding
   columns of numbers 37–38, 72
   headers and footers 60
   numeric values 114
   sort codes 66
addition 35
addresses 3
   block 12
adjusting
   column widths 28, 127
      automatically 29, 75
      with Auto Width 29
      with Fit button 91
   graph data series 100
   margins 60
   row height 29
aligning
   entries 127
   labels, with prefix characters 8
alignment
   buttons 127
   default 5
   of numeric values 8
Align Right button 113
#AND# 53, 79
application properties, Startup 16, 22, 132
applying styles 48
area graphs 95
arguments 39
   database @function 84
   text 54
arithmetic operators 35
arranging notebooks 17, 22
assigning
   macros to buttons 134–35
   names 40, 112
   passwords 16
asterisk (*) 10
automatic calculation 119
averages 40, 49
@AVG function 49
axes
   formatting 103
   labels 99

B

background calculation 119
bar graphs 93–94
   3-D 98
black blocks 127
block
   addresses 12
   Object Inspector 112, 117
   properties 28
      Column Width 29
      Data Entry Input 8, 11
      Font 45, 127
      Line Drawing 44, 127, 129
      Numeric Format 28, 38, 127
      Row Height 30
      Shading 127
      Text Color 127
blocks
   active cell in 12, 13
   copying 65
   extending without redefining names 112
   filling 67
   naming 40, 42
   output 80
   putting borders around 127, 129
   selecting 11

discontiguous 13, 127
  with Goto 13
  with keyboard 12
 shading 127
Bold button 45, 91, 127, 136
borders
 of graphs, changing 98
 printing 62
 putting around blocks 127, 129
budgets, setting up 90
buttons
 3 5
 @ 50
 Align Right 113
 alignment 127
 assigning macros to 134–35
 Bold 45, 91, 127, 136
 Close (Print Preview) 61
 Copy 20, 55, 65, 75, 91, 113
 creating 135
 Cut 22, 44
 Delete 26, 64
 Fit 29, 75, 91, 136
 Group 4, 83
 Insert 25, 36, 52, 55
 labeling 135
 Margin (Print Preview) 60
 Maximize 18, 23, 35
 notebook 128, 134
 Paste 20, 22, 44, 55, 65, 75, 91, 113
 Print (Print Preview) 61
 running macros with 135
 Setup (Print Preview) 59
 SpeedFill 66–67
 SpeedFormat 27, 117
 SpeedSort 68
 SpeedSum 37, 72
 SpeedTab 4, 102, 105
 X 5

C

calculating
 circular references 121
 formulas 122
  with F9 123
calculation
 area, creating 42
 automatic 119
 background 119
 manual 119
calculations
 simple 35
 using names in 51
canceling commands 14
cell
 active 4–5, 12–13
 addresses 3
 moving active 20
 references, absolute 57
 references, relative 56
 selector 5
@CELLPOINTER function 137
cells 3
 clearing 23
 deleting 26
 inserting 25
 moving 43
 naming 40–41, 136
 preformatting 45
 putting borders around 127, 129
 selecting 5
 shading 127
center prefix character (^) 8
changing
 color of text 127
 default directory 16
 entries 6, 19
 font size 45, 127
 graph
  borders 98
  colors 104
  types 94
 character styles 26
choosing
 commands 13
  with keyboard 13
CIRC indicator 122
circular references, calculating 121
Clear command 24
clearing
 cells 23
 vs. cutting 23
Clipboard 21
 displaying contents of 21
cloning notebooks 64
Close button (Print Preview) 61
Close command 35
closing
 notebooks 35
 Print Preview 61
color
 graph, changing 104
 text, changing 127
column graphs 95
Column Width property 29
column widths
 adjusting 28, 127
  automatically 29, 75
  with Auto Width 29
  with Fit button 91
 standard 10
columns
 inserting 24, 55
 selecting 12
combination graphs 95
Comma style 47
Comma0 style 47, 112, 114
commands 69
 Active Notebook 122, 132
 canceling 14
 choosing 13
  with keyboard 13

commands, *continued*
  Clear 24
  Close 35
  Copy 14, 19
  Copy (Block menu) 23
  Cut 14, 22
  Define Group 83
  Define Style 48
  Delete 105
  Exit 31
  Fill 65
  Goto 13
  Hide 18
  Insert 24
  Insert Break 59
  Keyboard 15
  Label Text 135
  Locked Titles 71
  Macro Debugger 139
  Macro Execute 128, 131
  Macro Record 129
  Macro Stop Record 129
  Macro Text 135
  Move 23
  Named Settings 62
  Names Create 40, 42, 52, 73, 75, 80, 112, 131, 133, 136
  New 17, 82, 90, 112, 117
  New View 18
  Open 35
  Page Setup 59
  Panes 72
  Paste 14, 19, 22
  Paste Special 86, 122
  Print 61
  Print Preview 57
  Printer Setup 58
  Query 74, 77
  Reformat 7
  Save 15
  Save All 87
  Save As 15–16, 64
  Series 100
  Show 18, 134
  Sort 68–70
  Tile 17, 22
  Titles 99
  Type 94
  Undo 20, 94
  Update Links 116
  Workspace Restore 117
  Workspace Save 117
comments in macros 130, 133
context-sensitive help 30
conventions
  field names 73–74
  filenames 16
Copy button 20, 55, 65, 75, 91, 113
Copy command 14, 19
Copy command (Block menu) 23
copying
  blocks 65
  entries 19, 113
    with Drag and Drop 21
  field names 75
  formulas 55, 91, 120
  graphs 101
  styles 47
  values only 86
correcting mistakes 6
@COUNT function 115
counting entries 115
creating
  buttons 135
  calculation area 42
  criteria table 75
  custom formats 50
  graph titles and labels 99
  graphics 96, 105
  groups 83
  invoices 126
  macros from scratch 132
multi-series graphs 93
new notebooks 16, 82, 90
notebook graphs 92, 105
output block 80
picture graphs 105
series
  of dates 65
  of numeric values 66
styles 48
criteria
  defining 74
  entering 76
  table 74, 75
curly braces ({ }) 128
Currency style 47, 48, 72, 91, 119, 120, 127
Currency0 style 47
Cut button 22, 44
Cut command 14, 22
cutting vs. clearing 23

D

Data Entry Input property 8, 11
data series 93, 100
database
  @functions 84
    arguments 84
    @DAVG 84–85
    @DCOUNT 84–85
    @DMAX 84, 86
    @DMIN 84, 86
    @DSUM 84–85
    vs. notebook @functions 84
  searches
    limiting 79
    repeating 79
Database Desktop 73
databases 72
  naming 73
  setting up 73
date formats 10, 127

Index

dates
   creating series of 65
   entering 10
      only 11
   formatting 28
   long 11
Date style 47
debugging macros 138
decimal places, setting 112, 113, 114
decision-making formulas 53
default alignment 5
Define Group command 83
Define Style command 48
defining
   criteria 74
   styles 48
Delete button 26, 64
Delete command 105
deleting 24
   cells 26
   graphs 93, 105
   records 79
   rows 64
designating end of spreadsheet 136
dialog boxes 14
directories
   changing default 16
   saving in different 16
displayed values 10, 49
displaying
   Clipboard contents 21
   data efficiently 42
   formulas 37
   hidden windows 18
   list of names 115
   long
      numeric entries 10
      text entries 6
   names 80
   SpeedBar 3
   status line 3

division 35
dollars and cents 38, 48, 72, 119, 120, 127
   negative 47
Drag and Drop editing 21, 43
Draw menu 105
drawing lines 44

E

editing
   activating input line 8
   Drag and Drop 21, 43
   notebooks 19
ellipsis (...) 14
ending macros 130
entering
   criteria 76
   dates 10
      only 11
   external references 85
   formulas 36
      from scratch 39
   @functions 39
   labels 4
      only 8
   numeric values 9
   references by pointing 40
   text 4
   times 10
entries
   aligning 127
   changing 6, 19
   copying 19
   counting 115
   erasing 23, 44
   moving 22
   pasting 20
      into different notebooks 22
   recording
      by clicking different cell 6
      with 3 button 5

      with Right Arrow 5
   right-aligning 113
   sorting 66
erasing entries 44
errors in macros 138
Exit command 31
expanding notebooks 18
extending block names 112
extensions, WB1 15
external references 115
extracting
   records 80
      unique 81

F

field names 73, 76
   conventions 73, 74
   copying 75
   including in database 74
fields 73
filenaming conventions 16
filling blocks 67
finding highest and lowest values 51
Fit button 29, 75, 91, 136
Fixed option 112, 113, 114
Fixed style 47
Font property 45, 127
fonts
   changing size of 127
   printer 46
footers, adding 60
formats
   custom 50
   date and time 10
formatting 26, 44
   character 26
   dates 28
   graph axes 103
   graph legends 104
   percentages 52
   quick, with SpeedFormat 27

formulas
  calculating 122
  copying 55, 91, 120
  decision-making 53
  displaying 37
  entering 36
    from scratch 39
  external references in 115
  pasting 91
  printing 62
  recalculating with F9 123
  referencing their cells 39
freezing labels 71
@Function list 49
@functions 35
  arguments 39
  @AVG 49
  @CELLPOINTER 137
  @COUNT 115
  database 84
    arguments 84
    @DAVG 84–85
    @DCOUNT 84–85
    @DMAX 84, 86
    @DMIN 84, 86
    @DSUM 84–85
    vs. notebook 84
  entering 39
  @HLOOKUP 118
  @IF 53
  @MAX 51
  @MIN 51
  nested 54
  @ROUND 114, 115
  @SUM 38, 114
  @VLOOKUP 118

G

getting help 30
giving instructions 13
Goto command 13
graph
  environment 102
  icons 106
    naming 105
  labels 93
  scale 94
Graph menu 95
Graph SpeedBar 102, 104
Graph tool 92, 93
graphics
  creating 96, 105
  importing and exporting 105
graphs
  adding data series 100
  area 95
  axis labels for 99
  bar 93, 94
    3-D 98
  changing
    borders 98
    colors 104
    type 94
  column 95
  combination 95
  copying 101
  creating
    multi-series 93
    on notebook 92
  data series 93
    adjusting 100
  deleting 93, 105
  formatting
    axes 103
    legends 104
  handles 93
  high-low 95
  labels 93
  large 101
  line 94, 97
  moving 95, 101, 105
  notebook
    creating 105
    formatting 98
  opening in windows 102
  picture 105
  pie 95
    multiple 96
  printing 107
  rotating 96
  scatter 95
  sizing 95, 105
  surface 95
  text 96
  titles for 99
  XY 95
Graphs page 4, 93
  moving to 102
Graphs Page SpeedBar 102, 104
Grid Lines property 131
gridlines
  printing 62
  turning off 131
Group button 4, 83
Group mode 83–84
grouping notebook
  pages 83
groups 82
  creating 83
  Quattro Pro for
    Windows 3

H

handles 93
headers, adding 60
Heading 1 style 47
Heading 2 style 47
help, context-sensitive 30
Hide command 18
hiding
  SpeedBar 15
  windows 18
high-low graphs 95
highest value, finding 51
@HLOOKUP function 118
horizontal lookup tables 118
hotlinks 87

I

icons
  graph 106
    naming 105
  Quattro Pro 2
@IF function 53
  nested 54
indicators, mode 4
input line 2
  activating 8
Insert Break command 59
Insert button 25, 36, 52, 55
Insert command 24
inserting 24
  cells 25
  columns 24, 55
  rows 25, 36, 52
insertion point 5, 19
invoices, creating 126
iteration 121

K

keyboard
  choosing commands
    with 13
  moving around with 20
  selecting blocks with 12
  shortcuts 15
    displaying list of 15
Keyboard command 15

L

Label Text command 135
labels
  aligning with prefix
    characters 8
  axis for graphs 99
  button 135
  distributing 7
  entering 4
    only 8
  freezing 71
  graph 93
  long 6
  for macros 130
  numbers as 7
  prefix characters 8
  repeating on printed
    pages 61
  and sorting 68
  unfreezing 72
left-align prefix character
  (') 8
legends, formatting 104
limiting database searches 79
Line Drawing property 44,
  127, 129
line graphs 94, 97
lines, drawing 44
linking
  with names 42
  notebooks 110, 115
    temporarily with
      groups 82
links, updating 87
locating records 76–77
Locked Titles command 71
logging invoices 136
long
  dates 11
  numeric entries 10
  text entries 6
looking up information 118
lookup tables 118
lowest value, finding 51

M

macro
  libraries 128, 132
    opening automati-
      cally 132
  names 128
  programming language
    126, 128
  recorder 128–29
  shortcut key 128, 131
Macro Debugger
  command 139
Macro Execute command
  128, 131
Macro Library property 132
Macro Record command 129
Macro Stop Record
  command 129
Macro Text command 135
macros 128
  assigning to buttons
    134–35
  comments in 130, 133
  creating from scratch 132
  ending 130
  errors in 138
  labels for 130
  naming 131, 133
  recording 128–29
  running 128
    with buttons 135
    with Macro Execute
      131
    with shortcut key
      131, 134
  startup 134
  stepping through 139
  stopping 132
  troubleshooting 138
  writing 132
manipulating
  notebooks 19
  records 74
  windows 17
manual calculation 119
Margin button (Print
  Preview) 60
margins, adjusting 60
@MAX function 51
Maximize button 18, 23, 35
menu bar 2, 13
menus 13
@MIN function 51

mistakes, correcting 6
mode indicators 4
mouse 2
   pointer shapes 6
Move command 23
moving
   active cell 5
   among matching records 78
   around a notebook 20
   cells 43
   to different page 4
   entries 22
      with Drag and Drop 23
   graphs 95, 101, 105
   to Graphs page 102
   pages 82
multiple
   notebooks 17
   pages, in one notebook 110
multiplication 35

N

Named Setting command 62
names
   assigning 40, 112
   in calculations 51
   displaying list of 80, 115
   extending block without redefining 112
   field 73, 76
   linking notebooks with 42
   macro 128
   using 41
Names Create command 40, 42, 52, 73, 75, 80, 131, 133, 136
naming
   blocks 40, 42
   cells 40–41, 136
   conventions 41
   criteria table 75

databases 73
graph icons 105
macros 131, 133
notebooks 15–16
output block 80
pages 81, 133, 136
print settings 62
negative dollar values 47
nested @functions 54
New command 17, 82, 90, 112, 117
New View command 18
Normal style 46, 55
#NOT# 53, 79
notebook
   active 17–18
   buttons 128, 134
   graphs
      creating 92, 105
      formatting 98
   links, updating 87
   Object Inspector 122
   pages 4
      grouping 83
   properties
      Macro Library 132
      Recalc Settings 119
      Zoom Factor 57
   statistics 3
   window 3
notebooks
   arranging 17, 22
   cloning 64
   closing 35
   creating new 16, 82, 90
   editing 19
   expanding 18
   formatting 44
   linking 110, 115
      with names 42
   moving around 20
   multiple pages in 110
   naming 15–16

opening
   existing 35
   new 112, 117
preserving previous version 16
previewing 57
printing 57
protecting with passwords 16
referencing other in formulas 115
saving 15
   as templates 127
   as workspaces 117
size of 3
working with multiple 17
numbers. *See* numeric values
Numeric Format property 28, 38, 112, 127
numeric values
   adding 114
   alignment of 8
   creating series of 66
   entering 9
   long 10
   rounding 114, 115
   totaling 37–38, 72
   treating as text 7

O

Object Inspectors 14
   application 16, 22, 132
   block 112, 117
   notebook 122
   opening 38
Open command 35
opening
   graphs in windows 102
   macro libraries automatically 132
   notebooks
      existing 35
      new 112, 117

Object Inspectors 38
windows 18
workspaces 117
operators 77, 79
arithmetic 35
list of 53
#OR# 53, 79
output block 80
naming 80
setting up 80
overlapping cut and paste areas 44

P

page
breaks 59
Graphs 4
moving to different 4
properties 131
tabs 4
pages
moving 82
multiple in one notebook 110
naming 81, 133, 136
notebook 4
Page Setup command 59
pane splitter 72
passwords, assigning 16
Paste button 20, 22, 44, 55, 65, 75, 91, 113
Paste command 14, 19, 22
Paste Special command 86, 122
pasting
entries 20
into different notebook 22
formulas 91
values only 122
Percent style 47, 52
picture graphs 105
pie graphs 95

multiple 96
prefix characters 8
preformatting cells 45
preserving previous notebook version 16
previewing notebooks 57
Print button (Print Preview) 61
Print command 61
Print Preview 57
closing 61
printing from 61
Print Preview command 57
print settings, naming 62
Printer Setup command 58
printing
from Print Preview 61
graphs 107
gridlines, borders, and formulas 62
labels on all pages 61
notebooks 57
number of copies 62
page block 62
page ranges 62
setting up pages for 59
protecting notebooks with passwords 16

Q

Quattro Pro
icon 2
quitting 31
starting 2–3
Query command 74, 77
quitting Quattro Pro 31

R

Recalc Setting property 119
recorder, macro 128–29
recording
by clicking different cell 6
macros 128–29

with 3 button 5
with Right Arrow 5
records 73
deleting 79
extracting 80
unique 81
locating 76–77
manipulating 74
moving among matching 78
references
absolute 57, 119–20
circular, calculating 121
entering by pointing 40
external 115
entering 85
relative 56
Reformat command 7
relative references 56
removing page breaks 59
repeating
database searches 79
labels on printed pages 61
resizing graphs 105
returning to original sort order 67, 73
revising notebooks 19
right-align prefix character (") 8
right-aligning entries 113
right-clicking 14
rotating graphs 96
@ROUND function 114, 115
rounding numeric values 114, 115
row height, adjusting 29
Row Height property 30
rows
deleting 64
inserting 25, 36, 52
selecting 12

running macros 128
    with buttons 135
    with Macro Execute 131
    with shortcut key 131, 134

S

Save All command 87
Save As command 15–16, 64, 69
Save command 15
saving
    all open notebooks 87
    in different directory 16
    with different name 16
    notebooks 15
        existing 16
    but preserving previous version 16
    print settings 62
    workspaces 117
scale of graphs 94
scatter graphs 95
scientific notation 10
scroll bars 4, 19
scrolling, synchronized 72
selecting
    blocks 11
        discontiguous 13, 127
        with Goto 13
        with keyboard 12
    cells 5
    columns 12
    rows 12
selector 5
Series command 100
setting
    date formats 127
    decimal places 112, 113, 114
    page breaks 59
setting up
    budget notebook 90
    databases 73
invoice log 136
    output block 80
    for printing 59
Setup button (Print Preview) 59
shading blocks 127
Shading property 127
shortcut key, macro 128, 131
Show command 18, 134
size
    of fonts, changing 45, 127
    of notebooks 3
sizing graphs 95
Slide Shows 104
Sort command 68–70
sort
    codes, adding 66
    order, returning to original 67, 73
sorting
    in descending order 70
    entries 66
    and labels 68
    on one key 67
    quickly with SpeedSort 68
    on three keys 70
    on two keys 69
    and wildcards 77
SpeedBar 2, 14
    displaying 3
    hiding 15
SpeedButton tool 128, 135
SpeedFill button 66, 67
SpeedFormat button 27, 117
SpeedSort button 68
SpeedSum button 37, 72
SpeedTab button 4, 102, 105
Split command 72
splitting windows 72
starting
    Quattro Pro 2–3
    Windows 2
startup macros 134
Startup property 16, 22, 132
status line 4
    displaying 3
stepping through macros 139
stopping macros 132
Style list box 46
styles 46
    applying 48
    character 26
    Comma 47
    Comma0 47, 112, 114
    copying 47
    Currency 47, 48, 72, 91, 119, 120, 127
    Currency0 47
    Date 47
    defining 48
    Fixed 47
    Heading 1 47
    Heading 2 47
    Normal 46, 55
    Percent 47, 52
    Total 47, 48
submenus 14
subtraction 35
@SUM function 38, 114
surface graphs 95
switching to another window 17
synchronized scrolling 72

T

tab scroller 4
table, criteria 74
tabs, page 4
telling Quattro Pro what to do 13
templates 127
text
    as @function arguments 54
    changing color of 127
    entering 4

Index

graphs 96
long entries 6
numbers as 7
Text Color property 127
Tile command 17, 22
time formats 10
times, entering 10
title bar 2, 16, 17
Titles command 99
titles for graphs 99
toolbar. *See* SpeedBar
tools
   Graph 92–93
   SpeedButton 128, 135
Total style 47, 48
Type command 94

U

underlying values 10, 49, 96
Undo command 20, 94
   turning on 22
undoing editing
     commands 20

unfreezing labels 72
Update Links command 116
updating notebook links 87
using names 41

V

values
   copying 86
   displayed 10
   finding highest and
     lowest 51
   pasting 122
   underlying 10, 96
vertical lookup tables 118
@VLOOKUP function 118

W

WB1 extension 15
wildcards, and sorting 77
windows
   displaying hidden 18
   hiding 18
   manipulating 17

moving among 17
notebook 3
opening new 18
splitting 72
Windows, starting 2
Workspace Restore
   command 117
Workspace Save
   command 117
workspaces 117
writing macros 132

X

X button 5
XY graphs 95

Z

Zoom Factor property 57
Zoom view 57
zooming in Print Preview 58

About the Authors

Joyce Cox
Before cofounding Online Press, Cox was Managing Editor of Microsoft Press. She is coauthor of six *Quick Course®* titles.

Patrick Kervran
Coauthor of *A Quick Course in Windows 3.1*, *A Quick Course in Lotus 1-2-3 for Windows*, and *A Quick Course in Excel 4 for Windows*, Kervran lives in Seattle, WA.

About Online Press

Founded in 1986, Online Press is a group of publishing professionals working to make the presentation and access of information manageable, efficient, accurate, and economical. In 1991 we began publishing our popular *Quick Course®* computer-book series, offering self-training for people with limited time to learn. At Online Press, it is our goal to help computer users quickly learn what they need to know about today's most popular software programs to get their work done efficiently.

Acknowledgments

Our thanks to Nan Borreson.

Cover design by Tom Draper Design
Interior design by Tom Draper Design, Joyce Cox, and Salley Oberlin
Graphics by Joyce Cox and Bill Teel
Word processing by Christina Smith
Proofreading by Polly Fox Urban
Layout by Joyce Cox and Bill Teel
Printed by Viking Press Inc.

Text composition by Online Press in Times Roman with display type in Avant Garde Gothic Bold, using Ventura Publisher and the Linotronic 300 laser imagesetter.

Printed on recycled paper

Other *Quick Course* Books

Don't miss the other titles in our *Quick Course*® series! Quality books at the unbeatable price of $12.95.

A Quick Course in Windows 3.1   ISBN 1-879399-14-8
A Quick Course in Excel 4 for Windows   ISBN 1-879399-15-6
A Quick Course in Word 2.0 for Windows   ISBN 1-879399-05-9
A Quick Course in Lotus 1-2-3 for Windows   ISBN 1-879399-07-5
A Quick Course in WordPerfect for Windows   ISBN 1-879399-06-7
A Quick Course in DOS 5   ISBN 1-879399-03-2
A Quick Course in WordPerfect 5.1   ISBN 1-879399-01-6
A Quick Course in Paradox for Windows   ISBN 1-879399-12-1 (Late 1992)

Plus more to come...

For a copy of our latest catalog, call us at (206) 641-3434 or write to us at:

Online Press Inc.
14320 NE 21st Street, Suite 18
Bellevue, WA 98007

Quick Course® books are distributed to bookstores in the U.S. by *Publishers Group West*, Emeryville, CA (510-658-3453 or 800-788-3123) and by *major wholesalers*; in Australia by *Step Up Systems* (03-427-0168); and in the United Kingdom by *Computer Bookshops Ltd*. (021-706-1188).